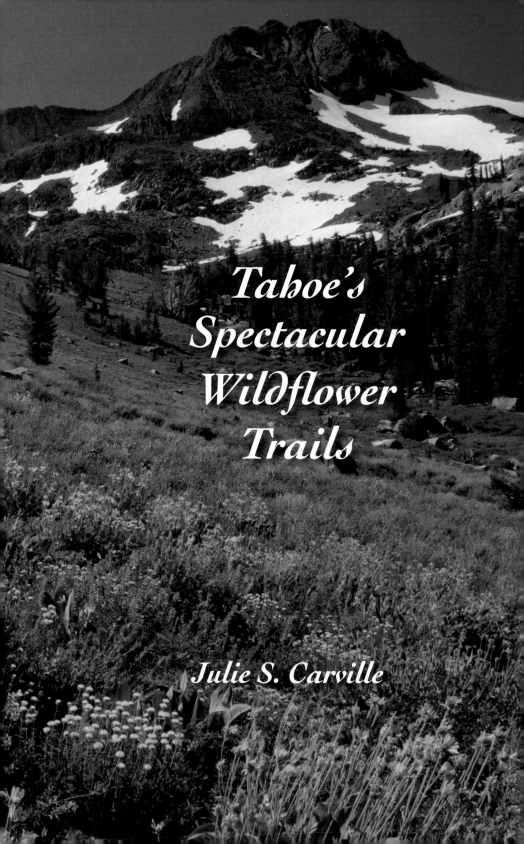

Tahoe's Spectacular Wildflower Trails

Julie S. Carville

Mountain Gypsy Press
P. O. Box 2618
Nevada City, CA 95959
mtngypsypress@gmail.com

© Copyright 2016 Mountain Gypsy Press

Library of Congress Control Number: 2016906766

ISBN: 978-0-692-69818-1

Design & Production: Joan Keyes, Dovetail Publishing Services
Cover Photo: "Trail up Basin Creek" Julie Carville
Pages ii–iii Photo: "Flowery slopes & Round Top Mountain" Julie Carville
Back Cover Photo: "From Basin Peak toward Castle Peak" Julie Carville
Photos: by Julie Carville unless otherwise credited
Maps: Charly Price

Disclaimer: Every effort has been made to confirm the accuracy of trail locations and descriptions. Please note that trailheads and trails may change over time. The Press and Author are not responsible for injury or any loss that may occur while using this book. Hikers must assume responsibility for their choices and actions by using common sense and good judgment regarding their abilities, the weather conditions, and their choice of trails for their safety and health as well as for their children.

Neither the Author nor Press can be held responsible for claims arising from using or ingesting plants as described in this book. Picking plants is against the law, and ingesting them without the knowledge to identify and safely process them can cause illness or death through allergic reaction or poisoning.

Summit of Mount Rose

Dedicated to my dear Rondal
who enriches my life
and shares my joy and love
for all that is wild and beautiful

Contents

A Note from the Author

The snow is falling outside my cabin window, covering the woods in a blanket of white. I feel excited by winter, as I watch the flakes drift slowly downward through the trees, but I must confess that my thoughts are on the thousands of little flowers sleeping away the winter beneath this protective covering. Years ago I moved to Tahoe and on one brisk morning in June, I walked out my back door down through the woods and came upon a huge meadow of yellow buttercups and purple violets. As I knelt down to look closely at a little monkeyflower, I discovered tiny rainbows sparkling in the dew drops on its small, silvery haired leaves. That morning changed my life, because it was the beginning of my commitment to make Tahoe's backcountry, and other wild places, an integral part of my life.

I wrote those words 27 years ago for my first wildflower book, *Lingering in Tahoe's Wild Gardens*, which was published in 1989. Through these many years, I've kept that commitment, which has taken me deeply into the flowers, nurturing and expanding me in ways I never thought possible. I've

Buttercups

Violets

loved flowers ever since I was a little girl as I planted petunias and pansies each spring in a place reserved for me in our family garden. So it was natural for me to share my love of wildflowers when I moved to Tahoe and lived among them. During these many years of leading wildflower classes and spending quiet time alone in the backcountry, I began to realize that flowers don't just bring us joy . . . they are also beings, who are just as alive as we are. They have much to teach us.

There have been many changes, since my first book. Peak wildflower displays are appearing at least a month earlier than normal, due to climate change. The science of plant genetics has brought new understandings of plant relationships, which has resulted in new plant families and name changes for many of the plants. In *Tahoe's Spectacular Wildflower Trails*, I've added hundreds of photos and a "Flowers by Color" section to help you identify the flowers. This new book includes some of the "old" hikes, because they are still Tahoe classics. Other hikes from my previous book have been dropped, when forests have invaded meadows or people have over-run the trails, and new fabulous hikes have been added.

Monkeyflower

While the essence of the book remains the same, over the past 27 years, I've had many new learnings and exhilarating experiences with Tahoe's wildflowers. I want to share all of this with you.

Dewdrops on Monkeyflower leaves

June 2016

A Blooming Overview

Guide to Using the Book

Each hike begins with "Featured Flowers" that are special or abundant along the trail and are bolded in the text to make them easy to find. To keep the book to a reasonable size for carrying in the field, I don't go into depth or provide photos for every flower mentioned on a hike. Use the "Flowers by Color" section to identify these.

The general blooming season is given for each trail, though climate change has made flowering times challenging to predict. Just know that after a heavy snow year, snows linger longer so blooming times may be a few weeks later; in a light snow year, they may bloom several weeks earlier.

The boot symbol  is just a guide; the difficulty or ease of a trail is really based on your acclimation to high elelvations, how often you hike, the conditions on the trail that day, and your enthusiasm.

In some years the snow lingers

The beginning and ending elevations do not take into account all the ups and downs, since those are mentioned on the hikes. In judging how long a hike will take, plan on about two miles per hour. This includes moderate ups and downs but not steep climbs or stops, and it doesn't apply to passionate botanists who want to say hi to every flower they meet along the trail or to the very young and elderly, who may have their own special pace.

Blooming Sequence

When I describe the flowers, don't expect them all to be in bloom at the same time. Some may be just starting to peek out of the soil, others will be in full bloom, and others may have already gone to seed.

In some years, the blooming of early-season flowers overlaps late-season flowers. Just like people, flowers don't fit into a tight, predictable schedule.

With that proviso, I can still say that spring generally arrives in Tahoe at the 6,200' lake level in May with the appearance of buttercups, camas lilies, and violets. The height of the wildflower season is generally from June through August. From late August through September blue gentians, red fuchsias, and yellow rabbitbrush bloom.

Bittercherry fruit

In late season to fall, plants are heavy with ripened fruit, and in October aspens turn golden to orange, with leaves that dance in the slightest breeze. By November, the world begins to quiet down as snow storms freeze and dust the wild gardens turning them into dull shades of yellow and brown. Soon the ground is frozen, and the plants become rumpled, listless reminders of once glorious days. This time of year used to sadden me, until I realized that the end of the flower season is just a time of rest in a reoccurring cycle that will bring new and dazzling displays of wildflowers in the coming spring.

Elderberry fruit

An Introduction to Tahoe

The Tahoe Sierra is in the northern half of the Sierra Nevada mountain range. The Washoe people of western Nevada came to Lake Tahoe each summer to live and fish by its vast shoreline, until the early 1900s. They honored their lake as a sacred Being, who nurtured them. Its clear waters are surrounded by majestic conifered mountains; changing weather can turn the water from deep, rich blue to turquoise. John Muir named the Sierra's

From the east side of Lake Tahoe

awe-inspiring mountains "The Range of Light." At dawn, their granitic peaks glow pink, and later they shine with alpenglow as the sun is setting.

The Tahoe area covers many square miles and is divided into different National Forests and protected wilderness areas with various

The waters near Sand Harbor

management units. Lake Tahoe is the largest of all the Sierra Nevada's lakes; few lakes in the world are as large or as deep. It is 22 miles long, 12 miles wide, and 1,640' at its deepest. If all the water it now holds were to cover California, the state would be under 14" of water. More than 60 streams flow into the lake, but there is only one outlet, the Truckee River.

Brief Geologic History

Lake Tahoe lies in a basin that began forming at least 33 million years ago. According to Jeffrey Schaffer, author of *The Tahoe Sierra*, lava flowed in episodes over eons of time from Mt. Pluto near Tahoe's north shore. About 2¼ million years ago, the lake began to form as rain, melting snow, and inlet streams started filling the basin. Over more time, immense glaciers dammed its water up to 600' above its present level of 6,229'. With water pressure building up against the glacier dam, the waters broke through forming a huge river that has since subsided into what we now call the Truckee River. It flows through Tahoe City to Truckee and then east through Reno to finally rest in Pyramid Lake. The massive glaciers also slowly moved down canyons on the west side of the lake scouring granite hillsides and moving loose rock downhill to change V-shaped canyons into U-shaped valleys. As the glaciers pushed loose rocks to the side, moraines were formed, and as the glaciers melted over time, bays, lakes, and glacially polished granite walls and ridges were left exposed with random boulders deposited along the way.

The M. S. Dixie II cruises into Emerald Bay

Flowers along the Big Meadow trail

An Exceptional Botanical Community

Tahoe provides a home for a rich botanical community, within a state known for its large variety of plants. There are more native plants in California than in the northeastern and central United States combined. At least 6,000 plant species, subspecies, and varieties are known to grow in California, and one third of California's native plants grow only in California. This rich plant diversity is due in part to a complex mix of granitic, volcanic, and metamorphic rocks that have decomposed to create a variety of soil types. It's also the result of plants migrating up the western flanks of the Sierra and up from the eastern Great Basin to meet and mix at Tahoe.

A Special Consideration

We will be journeying through glorious gardens of wildflowers and though it may be tempting to pick them, please leave them for others to enjoy. One

Mariposa Lily

day as I hiked down a trail, I came upon a forlorn pile of wildflowers that had been discarded, after they wilted. Most wildflowers plucked from their wild gardens soon wither in body and spirit. If you want to examine a flower, don't just casually pick it, look at it, and then drop it when you are done. Instead, kneel down to meet your plant at its own level, on its own terms. Enjoying flowers in this way will honor the preciousness of their lives and deepen your experience.

Botany & the Miracle of Plants

You soon realize that in strolling in the meadows in the merry month of May you are witnessing an orgy of sex beside which La Dolce Vita is like a bishop's garden party.

—Adrian Bell

Adrian Bell's comment is a light hearted reminder that flowers are just glorious collections of reproductive organs, brightly and unabashedly announcing their availability to neighboring insects or carelessly casting their fate to the wind. A flower's function, besides that of creating joy in our hearts, is reproduction. Each flower is generally made up of four basic structures: green sepals that enclose the flower in bud, colorful petals to attract pollinators, and both male and female

Clarkias

reproductive parts. The stems, leaves, and roots support and nourish the flowers as they go about their important business of creating new little bundles of joy.

How Reproduction Occurs

The female pistil produces seeds, and the male stamen produces pollen. The pistil is composed of 3 parts: the ovary, style, and stigma. The ovary sits in the flower's center and houses the ovules, which after fertilization mature into seeds. The style rises out of the ovary and supports the stigma, which is the part that receives pollen. The stamen is composed of only 2 parts: a filament and an anther. The filament supports the anther, and the anther produces the pollen in a little sac-like structure. As in humans, the male is simpler, but just as important!

Camas Lily

When the pollen grains are mature and ready to fertilize other flowers, their little sacs open to expose their pollen grains, which are then dispersed by birds, insects or the wind. When the ovules are ready to be fertilized, the stigma opens and exudes a mucilaginous substance. After pollen is deposited on a stigma, each pollen grain germinates in that substance and grows a tube-like structure, nurtured by the style, until the tube reaches the ovary. After the tube enters the ovary, sperm cells are released from the tip and unite with an ovule, which matures into a seed. This process must occur for every seed that forms. Ovaries are in many different forms. They include vegetables (which botanists call fruits) like pea pods, corn, string beans, tomatoes, as well as rose hips, berries, apples and all other fruits. After fertilization, the petals usually fall off, and the ovary swells, until it bursts open to release its seeds onto the soil to give birth to new plants.

The Foundation of All Life

Through the miracle of flowers, plants reproduce themselves but through the miracle of photosynthesis, they convert the energy of sunlight into carbohydrates. In doing so they sustain all other life on this planet. The Washoes and other indigenous people respected plants as life sustaining beings who gave up their lives so the Washoe could live. They honored plants as little "brothers and sisters" who were different but equal in the scheme of life. Too often plants and animals are put into a hierarchy, with humans at the top. Yet it is the green plants that produce the carbohydrates, food, and oxygen needed to sustain our lives. This counters the common assumption that humans should be at the top of the hierarchy, though I see no value in comparing life forms in a hierarchy.

In his book, *The Power of Plants*, Brendan Lehane expands our appreciation of plants. He writes, "Plants have the power to . . . break rocks,

staunch floods, precipitate rain, or knit sand to resist the buffets of the sea. After catastrophes of fire, eruption, hurricane, and avalanche they can rise again, like the phoenix, to retrace their patient progress across the land. To procreate their species they have enslaved whole races of insects. To spread themselves they enlist wind, sea, and animals as porters. No man can garner sunbeams, or commit his off-spring to the wind for a journey of a thousand miles. A dandelion can. Science has far to go before it matches the ingenuity of a wayside weed."

A dandelion releasing its seed

The Development of Botany

Botany, or the study of plants, has developed gradually over thousands of years. Early people grouped plants by food, medicine, shelter, and clothing. Early physicians became botanists to study plants for medicinal preparations and later classified them by their medicinal qualities. Theophrastus (370–285 B.C.), a student of Aristotle, was the first person known to have left written records of systematic plant classification. For the next 2,000 years, written plant knowledge was preserved in herbals according to their economic and medicinal uses.

A Shocking Discovery

The Swedish botanist, zoologist, and physician Carl Linnaeus (1707–1778) made the startling discovery that plants reproduced sexually, which horrified many in the religious community. One outraged minister claimed such a concept could only have come from a "grossly prurient mind" but in time, the scientific community recognized the truth of his observations and honored him for his discovery. He also developed a system of plant classification that was based on the number of sexual organs in a flower. Linnaeus knew that his system was only a convenient way of grouping plants, until another system was later developed. Botanists now classify plants by their shared evolutionary development based on genetics. Scientific nomenclature is in the form of Latinized words, because this was the language of scientists when Linnaeus first developed the binary system that we now use.

The System of Plant Names

There are at least 400,000 species of flowering plants throughout the world, and there are perhaps thousands of plants in tropical climates or other remote areas that have yet to be discovered.

To name plants has been a formidable task, and prior to Linnaeus there was no consistent nomenclature, so plants carried cumbersome names of five or more words. His system of two Latin names for each plant enabled botanists to organize plants and communicate with other botanists locally and in other countries, in a systematic and easily understood language.

Violet (Viola macloskeyi)

For instance, there are many violets throughout the world, but there is only one type or species of violet with the name "*Viola macloskeyi."* The first word *"Viola"* is the genus, which is a group of closely related species that have specific characteristics in common. *"Viola macloskeyi"* is an individual species name. Occasionally in describing a species, I'll use "sub species" (ssp.)" or "variety" (var.)," which are terms to describe a noticeable difference in certain plants within the same species. These differences can occur when a plant adapts to a changing habitat. Plants are also grouped by families, which are composed of numerous genera, just as one genus is made up of one or more species.

Oh, Those Awful Latin Names!

For the sake of consistency, I use botanical and common names based on *The Jepson Manual, Vascular Plants of California*, 2nd edition, 2012. When the manual doesn't provide common names, I have chosen the names most commonly used by Tahoe's botanists. Learning the names of wildflowers helps us to feel better acquainted with them, and most people initially have little interest in ever learning their Latin names. Many are content with common names, since they are charming and easier to remember, but common names can be confusing, when the same plants in different places have different common names.

For botanists from different regions or countries this confusion would make it difficult to impossible to discuss plants. Botanical names seem complicated, because Latin is unfamiliar to us, but once we start using them they can become familiar. For example *"Geranium,"* is a Latin genus that has become a household word. Latin names also give us interesting information about a flower's structure, habitat or other aspects. The botanical name for the Buttercup genus is *"Ranunculus."* This is a word derived from Latin for "little frog," because buttercups usually share wet habitats with these little creatures.

An Introduction to Several Plant Families

Learning plants by family helps us to group plants into a grid system to organize and study them. Since the complex field of plant genetics has developed, it is harder now to identify plants in the field, by easily observable flower forms, and we can't check out their genes in the field to confirm their identity! Many similar plants, which were thought to be in the same family, have now been grouped into many different plant families, even though they may share many structual similarities. For this reason, I don't focus on plant families, but the Sunflower, Pea, and Violet Families are easy to recognize, at least by their families in the field.

Sunflower Family

Daisy form

Thistle form

Dandelion form

Mule's Ears phyllaries

Alpine Aster phyllaries

Arrowleaf Butterweed fluffy pappus

The Sunflower Family has evolved into three different flower forms: the Daisy with bisexual disk flowers *and* female ray flowers, the Thistle with bisexual disk flowers *only,* and the Dandelion with bisexual ray flowers *only.* All of these flowers are held in cup-like phyllaries, and most of them have seeds attached to pappus that fluffs out, as the seeds mature to distribute them by the wind. See pp. 154–155.

Pea Family flowers are made up of 5 petals: an upper banner petal with markings to attract insects, 2 side petals, called "wings," that cover 2 fused

Pea Family

Typical Pea (lupine) flowers

Lupine peapods

spur

Long-spurred Violet

Roger Rosenberger

A curious little penstemon!

petals, which are called a keel that encloses the stamens and one pistil. Their ovules mature inside recognizable peapods. See p. 241.

Violet Family flowers are easy to recognize. They have 2 upper petals without nectar lines and 2 side petals and a larger lower petal that are marked with nectar lines and hairs. A nectar spur extends backward from the base of the petals. See pp. 67–69. It isn't usually this simple to identify flowers, but it can be fun to begin using a plant key to identify flowers.

What Is a Plant Key?

A plant key is a binary system that compares a plant's "key features" to identify flowers. At each stage in the key, there are two choices: does it have 4 petals or 5 or more petals, are its petals white or pink, is the plant up to 12″ tall or taller than 12″? Until finally you arrive at the name of the little flower that is sitting there "curiously" looking up at you, wondering what in the world you're doing!

Though it sounds clear cut, the actual process, even for a trained botanist, can be frustrating. There are many reasons for this, but the main thing to realize is that using keys can be fun and useful for budding botanists too, because they are a helpful way to learn botanical terms, and they sensitize us to the lovely details of flowers. Of course, a problem for the beginning botanist is the seemingly complicated terminology. Many a beginner has been frustrated by a description like "lvs. canescent, pinnatifid with linear-filiform subterete divisions" or confused by the many different terms botanists use just to describe the shape and growth patterns of hairs on a leaf. I have minimized botanical terms in the book, but have included a small glossary when it would be helpful.

Another help in learning to key out plants is to know a few basic leaf forms. Leaves are either simple with smooth edges or their edges are lobed, serrated or in some other form. Other leaves are compound, which means

Simple leaf

Simple leaf, lobed & serrated

Compound palmate leaf

Compound pinnate leaf

each leaf is so deeply lobed to its midvein that it is made up of many smaller leaves, called leaflets. Compound leaves come in two forms. A compound palmate leaf is composed of leaflets that radiate outward from a central point, like fingers from the palm of a hand. A compound pinnate leaf has leaflets arranged in parallel rows, like a ladder with a middle axis.

If keying out flowers, learning their common or Latin names, and studying the processes in flowers help you to more deeply connect with them, then that's wonderful. If your way is to daydream in a meadow of wildflowers and never learn a name, that's fine too. My way is to combine knowledge and daydreaming. I believe that knowledge without soul is empty, while soul with knowledge helps to enrich our relationship with all that surrounds us.

Are Plant Intelligent?

> *There are two equally dangerous extremes — to shut reason out, and*
> *to let nothing else in.*
>
> — Pascal (1623–1662)

We've been taught that plants are pretty, though of course not intelligent, but Stephen Buhner in his extraordinary book, *Plant Intelligence, and the Imaginal Realm*, writes, "Plants in fact, possess a highly sophisticated neural system and while it does not look like our "brain" it really is, in actuality, a brain. In fact, once you get over brain chauvinism, it's not all that different from our own."

Dictionaries define intelligence as the ability to learn, understand or deal with new or trying situations. It also refers to the ability to apply knowledge to manipulate one's environment. Scientists have been discovering that plants, and indeed all other life forms, exhibit these abilities and more. It's beyond the scope of this book to explore this deeply, but Buhner's book will take you on an exciting journey that will awaken you in new ways to expand your relationship with plants.

You'll learn that the roots of plants function like our brains, with many of the same hormones and chemicals that are also produced in humans. You'll learn that these substances were in plants and animals millions of years before humans appeared. Plant root-brains are composed of neurons (brain cells) and axons (brain cell transmitters and connecters) like human brains. Though plant brains appear different, they perform many of the same functions as our brains. They cooperate to help the same species or other species to survive, they make choices, and they have memory. Plants protect themselves with substances, which they produce to deter predators. A great example is a bean plant that analyzes the saliva of a specific species of spider mite, as it is nibbling on its leaves. The plant remembers the predator and responds by mixing substances in the right preportions to create a specific pheromone. It releases the pheromone into the environment to attract the exact predator that eats that specific mite species. The pheromone also stimulates other bean plants to start producing the same pheromone to protect themselves.

Dr. Suzanne Simard, a Forest Ecologist and professor from the University of British Columbia, studies the vast, symbiotic relationships between soil fungi that attach themselves to trees and other plants in complex inter-relationships in a forest. She used radioisotopes to track carbon, water, and nitrogen that was being exchanged between an elder Douglas Fir (Mother tree) and a Paper Birch. After Simard shaded the Birch tree, so it couldn't photosynthesize, the Mother Douglas Fir sent out carbon-based sugars through soil fungi to sustain the Birch. Mother trees favor their own offspring in such exchanges, but they also sustain other trees. Scientists are finding that these fungal-plant networks interconnect large plant communities to cooperatively exchange nutrients or to warn of predators. We are finding that the norm isn't ruthless competition but a system of symbiosis that supports the whole community of trees and other plants,

Western Polemonium

which is discussed further on some of the hikes. It would be life changing if our capitalistic society embraced the level of cooperation that we see everywhere in plant communities.

This isn't the only way that plants communicate. According to Buhner, "Plants also speak using auditory signals through a complex, sound-based language that is far more ancient than our human one, though it exists in a more subtle sound-spectrum than our own." The Ecologist Richard Karban, who teaches at the University of California at Davis is learning the language of Sagebrush plants that speak to one another in the Northern Sierra. As he listens in, he is "beginning to understand what they say."

Plants have a consciousness and a brain crucial to their survival, just as ours is. I find it odd that it is difficult for some scientists to even consider this, and yet they belittle other scientists who scientifically do research in this area. I'm grateful for curious scientists like Einstein, Suzanne Simard, Nobel Prize winner Barbara McClintock and others who are willing to think outside the box. It is such exploratory thinking that has helped us to realize a wider, wiser, and more beautiful world.

All plants, animals, birds, insects, and even bacteria are aware beings, sharing the mystery of life with us. Pythagoras, the Greek philosopher and mathematical genius who lived from 570–495 B.C., is said to have exclaimed, "Astonishing! Everything is Intelligent!"

Preparing for Your Day

The lighter your load the happier you'll be in life and on on the trail, so I recommend minimum baggage:

❀ A compass and maps, because over time trails can change or signs may disappear, making decisions at trail junctures difficult. I've suggested maps from www.adventuremaps.net (AM) or National Geographic Maps from www.trailsillustrated.com (NG).

❀ The U. S. Forest Service at Tahoe's north or south shore can tell you if the trails are free of snow and provide updated information on day and overnight permits, which are required for Desolation Wilderness. Some permits require fees and others don't, and this can change over time.

❀ Water is a must. If there are lakes or streams on the hike, carrying a water filter reduces weight and protects against giardia, a microscopic organism present in some Sierra streams, which can cause severe intestinal disorders.

❀ Plant-based insect repellent instead of toxic alternatives.

❀ A 10-Power hand lens (magnifying glass) is really fun and can be purchased through universities, rock shops or nature stores. The Earth Store in Nevada City, California, 530-265-0448, www.earthstorenc.com, is a good source. One look through a high quality lens, and you'll be

hooked on exploring the detail of every flower, leaf, and insect. Cheap magnifying glasses will only discourage you, because they lack clarity and have insufficient magnification. I use a Bausch & Lomb 10-powered lens, to which I can attach a cord for carrying it around my neck, so I don't lose it.

- Clothing selection is personal, but I dress in layers to adjust to weather changes. I wear hiking sandals or other lightweight hiking shoes for comfort and a hat and sunglasses. A waterproof rain jacket is also important.

- Personal items, such as sun screen, chapstick, lunch, and of course toilet paper. Please bury "it" using common sense where you go (at least 100' from a stream). Better yet, carry paper and "it" out in a plastic bag.

- A treat is an ice chest with cold drinks for the hike's end, covered or in the trunk, so a bear doesn't break into your car.

Do as I say, not as I do! You may want to lighten your load.

Sulfur Fungus on a dying White Fir

Tahoe's Trees

Pine Family (Pinaceae)

Firs

Abies genus, each needle is single on branches, needles lack fascicles (see below), cones upright like Christmas tree candles

Red Fir needles are solid green

Red Fir's (Abies magnifica), *tightly clustered needles near top of tree are like a snowflake*

White Fir needles less dense than in Red Firs and whitish to light green at base

White Firs (Abies concolor), *upright, 3–5" long cones resemble Red Fir cones*

Red Fir with upright cones 6–9" long

19

Pines

Pinus genus, bundle of needles sheathed at the base held in a brown papery fascicle, attached to the branch, cones hang down

Pine Cones compared

2 needles in a fascicle:

Lodgepole male cones and mature female cone

Lodgepole, female's young cones will mature into brown, woody cones

Lodgepole Pine (Pinus contorta *ssp.* murrayana), *cones about 2" long*

3 needles in a fascicle:

Jeffrey Pine needles

Jeffrey Pine (Pinus jeffreyi), *cones 5–10" long*

Jeffrey Pine, shaped by age

Jeffrey Pine young cones top, mature cones below

Ponderosa Pine

Ponderosa Pine needles

Washoe Pine, Pinus ponderosa *var: washoensis, cones 2–4" long, uncommon tree, grows on east slope of Mount Rose, in Galena Creek watershed*

5 needles in a bundle:

Sugar Pine (Pinus lambertiana), *cones 10–20" long*

Western White Pine (Pinus monticola), *cones 5–12" long*

Sugar Pines have the largest cones

Sugar Pines have the thinnest needles

Western White Pine, mature & young cones

Western White Pine mature cone

5 needles in a bundle:

Whitebark Pine,
male pollen cones

Whitebark Pine (Pinus albicaulis), *cones 1½–3" long*

Whitebark Pine, female cones

Hemlocks

Tsuga genus, single needles grow on branches, cones hang down

Mountain
Hemlock
needles,
younger
needles are
light green

Mountain
Hemlock
cone

Mountain Hemlock (Tsuga mertensiana),
cones 1–3" long, treetops nod

Cypress Family (Cupressaceae)

Cedars & Junipers

needles parallel to branches and compressed

Incense Cedar female cones, woody with "wings," male pollen cones at tips of needles

Incense Cedar (Calocedrus decurrens), *needles parallel to branches, overlapping, flattened, grows up to 7,000' elevations*

Sierra Juniper female blue cones, berry-like

Sierra Juniper (Juniperus grandis), *needles parallel to branches and appressed*

Willow Family (Salicacea)

Black Cottonwoods on South Fork of Yuba River, Donner Pass area

Black Cottonwood leaves

Black Cottonwoods (Populus trichocarpa)
starting to turn color

Aspen leaves

Quaking Aspens (Populus tremuloides)

Aspens turn yellow in fall

Aspens also turn a brilliant orange in fall

Flowers by Color

Some same flower species bloom in more than one color. This is indicated by the color initials by the flower's name: W for white or creamy, Y for yellow or golden, Pk for pink, P for purple, L for lavender, R for Red, G for Green. Blue and purple flowers can be bluish purple. Flower colors change after fertilization. Flower images are not to scale. All photos are by the author, unless labeled with another photographer's initials in parentheses: Steve Ashcraft (SA), Lisa Berry (LB), Geoff Griffin (GG), Roger Rosenberger (RR).

WHITE to CREAM

Alpine Cryptantha

Alpine Gentian

Alpine Knotweed

Alpine Paintbrush
W, Y, Pk

Bear Buckwheat

Bistort

Bittercherry

Bog Saxifrage

Brewer's Angelica

Brook Saxifrage
(LB)

Bud Saxifrage   (LB)

Bush Chinquapin

Butterballs

California
Hesperochiron

California Mountain
Ash

California Skullcap

California Valerian

Cassiope

Chickweed

Corn Lily

Coulter's Fleabane

Cow Parsnip

Cream Bush

Creek Dogwood

Cushion Phlox

Cut-leaf Fleabane

Davis' Knotweed   G

Douglas' Catchfly

Drummond's Anemone

Dusky Horkelia

Dwarf
Chamaesaracha

Dwarf Everlasting

Dwarf Lewisia

Dwarf Onion

False Soloman's Seal, Star-flowered

False Soloman's Seal, Western

Fivespot

Globe Gilia

Grass of Parnassus

Grass of Parnassus, Fringed

Gray's Lovage

Hooded Lady's Tresses

Hot-rock Penstemon

King's Sandwort (RR)

Labrador Tea

Leichtlin's Mariposa Lily

Lemmon's Catchfly (RR)

Little Prince's Pine

Lobb's Buckwheat

Macloskey's Violet

Marsh Marigold

Meadow Thistle

Miniature Gilia	Miniature Lotus Pk	Mitten-leaf Nemophila	Mountain Sagebrush
Needle Navarretia	Nevada Lewisia	Nude Buckwheat	One-sided Wintergreen G
Parish's Yampah (GG)	Pinemat Manzanita	Plainleaf Fawn Lily	Plumas Ivesia
Potbelly Owl's Clover	Prickly Phlox Pk, L	Ranger's Buttons	Richardson's Geranium

Sand Corn	Shasta Knotweed	Sierra Claytonia Pk	Sierra Mariposa Lily

Sierra Saxifrage

Slender Bird's Beak

Slender Paintbrush
Y

Staining Collomia
P

Sugar Stick

Thimbleberry

Three-leaved Lewisia

Tobacco Brush

Tuber Starwort

Utah Serviceberry

Washington Lily

*Western
False-asphodel*

*Western Pasque
Flower*

*White-flowered Bog
Orchid*

White Hawkweed

*White-veined
Wintergreen   (RR)*

Whitethorn

Wright's Buckwheat

Yarrow

Alpine Buttercup

Alpine Gold

Alpine Lily

Alpine Sagewort

Arrowleaf Butterweed

Arrow-leaved
Balsamroot

Baker's Violet

Bigleaf Avens

Bitterbrush

Brewer's Cinquefoil

Brewer's Golden Aster

California Sunflower

California Wavewing

Canada Goldenrod

Club-moss Ivesia

Clustered Broomrape
Pk

Comb Draba

Fan Violet

Fanleaf Cinquefoil

Frosted Wild
Buckwheat

Gordon's Ivesia

Graceful Cinquefoil

Hairy Arnica

Heartleaf Arnica

Lance-leaf Stonecrop

Large-flowered
Collomia

Lemmon's Keckiella

Miniature Tarweed

Mountain Mule's Ears

Mountain Violet

Mt. Rose Wild
Buckwheat

Musk Monkeyflower

Nodding Microseris

Pinewoods Lousewort

Plantain Buttercup

Pretty Face

Primrose
Monkeyflower

Rocky Mountain
Butterweed

Seep-spring
Monkeyflower

Shaggy Hawkweed

Sibbaldia

Silky Raillardella

Single-stem Butterweed

Sticky Cinquefoil

Stream Violet

Sulphur Flower

Tinker's Penny

Tuberous Sanicle

Twinberry

Western Buttercup

Western Sweet Cicely

Western Wall Flower

Woolly-flowered Gooseberry

Woolly Groundsel

Woolly Sunflower

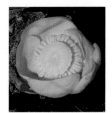

Yellow Pond Lily

Alpine Dusty Maidens

Alpine Shooting Stars

Anderson's Thistle

Bleeding Heart

Bog Laurel

Bog Mallow

Brewer's
Monkeyflower

Creeping Snowberry

Dwarf Monkeyflower
Y

Elephant's Head

Elephant's Head,
Little

Fireweed

Graceful Phlox

Greenleaf Manzanita

Hairy Paintbrush

Kelloggia

Lemmon's Paintbrush

Lewis' Monkeyflower

Long-petaled Lewisia
W

Mountain Heather

Mountain Pink
Currant

Mountain Pride

Mountain Rose

Mountain Spiraea

Narrow-tube
Skyrocket

Pink Alumroot

Pink Star Onion

Prairie Smoke
W, R, Y

Pussypaws

Rock Fringe

Rosey Pussytoes

Round Leaf Snowberry

Ruby Sand Spurry

Self Heal L

Sierra Bilberry

Sierra Onion

Sierra Primrose

Sierra Shooting Star

Spanish Lotus

Spreading Dogbane

Spring Beauty W

Staining Collomia

Steer's Head

Sticky Currant

Swamp Onion

Torrey's Monkeyflower

Wax Currant W

Western Snakeroot (SA)

Whisker Brush

White-veined Mallow

RED

Brown's Peony

California Fuchsia

Crimson Columbine

Double Honeysuckle

Giant Red Paintbrush

Rosy Sedum

Scarlet Gilia

Sheep Sorrel

Sierran Gooseberry

Snow Plant

Spotted Coral Root Orchid

Wavy-leaved Paintbrush

Western Prickly Gooseberry

BLUE to LAVENDER to PURPLE

Alpine Aster

American Speedwell

Azure Penstemon

Ballhead Phacelia

Beckwith's Violet

Blue Flax

Blue-eyed Grass

Blue-eyed Mary

Brewer's Lupine

Cusick's Speedwell

Dagger Pod

Explorer's Gentian

Hiker's Gentian	*Hoary Aster*	*Horsemint*	*Jacob's Ladder*
Large-leaf Lupine	*Leichtlin's Camas Lily*	*Long-spurred Violet*	*Low Phacelia*
Lyall's Dwarf Lupine	*Mahala Mat*	*Meadow Penstemon*	*Monkshood W, Pk*
Mountain Bluebells	*Mountain Jewelflower W*	*Mountain Larkspur*	*Mountain Pennyroyal (Coyote Mint) W*

Naked Broomrape Y	*Naked Mariposa Lily*	*Nuttall's Larkspur*	*Pine Lupine W, Y*

Porterella	*Pursh's Woolly Pod*	*Quamash Camas Lily*	*Self Heal*
Shining Fleabane W	*Showy Penstemon (RR)*	*Showy Polemonium*	*Slender Navarretia*
Slender Penstemon	*Spreading Phlox W, Pk*	*Spurred Lupine*	*Star Lavender*
Stickseed, Jessica's	*Stickseed, Sierran*	*Tahoe Lupine*	*Thyme-leaved Veronica*

Timberline Phacelia	*Torrey's Blue-eyed Mary*	*Torrey's Lupine*	*Wandering Daisy*

Wavy-leaved Aster

Western Aster

Western Blue Flag

Western Polemonium

Western Waterleaf
W   (RR)

Whitney's Locoweed
W

Whorled Penstemon

GREEN

Brewer's Bishop's Cap
(LB)

Davis' Knotweed

Fendler's Meadow Rue,
female

Fendler's Meadow Rue,
male

Monument Plant
(Green Gentian)

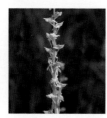

Sparsley-flowered Bog
Orchid   W

Western Sweet Cicely

Tahoe's Hike Locations

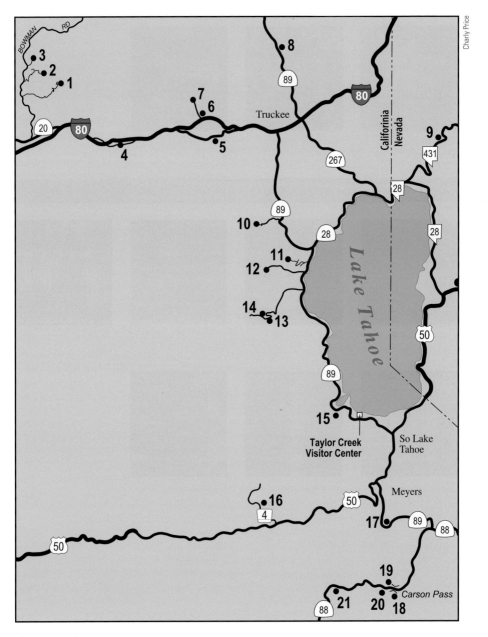

#1 Sanford Lake

Sanford Lake

One Way: 0.5 mile
Trail Begins/Ends: 7,400'/7,058'
Map: NG: Tahoe National Forest, Sierra Buttes/Donner Pass
Wildflower Season: late May through August

Sanford Lake offers great swimming with stunning, long distance views and gorgeous summer and fall hiking. The lake is reached on a short, downhill trail that doesn't feel short, because there are so many flowers along the hillsides, in creekside gardens, and by the lake. This easy trail allows plenty of time to enjoy the wildflowers with a hand lens for a deep look into the beauty of their world. The lake is especially spectacular, because its waters rest in a bowl that is backdropped by a sheer rock wall with grassy wildflower gardens at its base.

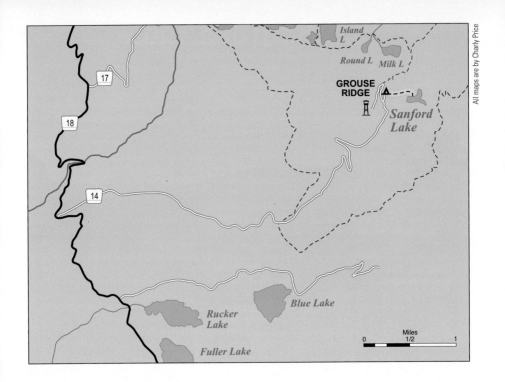

Featured Flowers

Plainleaf Fawn Lily (*Erythronium purpurescens*)
Spreading Phlox (*Phlox diffusa*)
Single-stem Butterweed (*Senecio integerrimus*)
Mountain Jewelflower (*Streptanthus tortuosus*)
Sierra Bilberry (*Vaccinium caespitosum*)
Star-flowered False Solomon's Seal (*Maianthemum stellatum*)

Trailhead Directions: **Drive west from Donner Summit or east from Colfax** on Highway 80. Take the Highway 20 exit and drive west on Highway 20 for 4.5 miles. Turn right onto Bowman Lake Road by the wooden shacks. **From Nevada City** at the intersection of Highways 20 and 49, head east on Highway 20 for 25.5 miles and turn left at Bowman Lake Road and the shacks. The turnoff is after the large, unsigned Bear Valley. Drive another 6.4 miles and turn right onto Grouse Ridge Road (FR #14). Drive another 5.9 miles to a road split to turn right into the campground. (The road heading uphill at the split leads to the ridgeline.) Picnic tables are provided at the campsites but not water or garbage facilities. Camping is free and first come, first served. Please don't park by campsites for day use.

The long drive in is worth it for the beauty of the flowers and the lake. The ridgeline above the campground has distant vistas, parking for other hikes, and a steep road that leads up to an old lookout tower at 7,711'. The lookout was built in 1923, closed down in the mid 1970s but will be available for short-term vacation rentals, when the renovation is completed. Contact the Yuba River Ranger District at 530-288-3231.

Lookout Tower seen from Island Lake

The trail begins in the lower campsite area by the Sanford Lake sign. Grouse Ridge is named after the Blue Grouse, a large bird now called "Sooty Grouse" for its dark brown feathers. Grouse inhabit shrubby coniferous forests. Some remain in the mountains at Sagehen Creek throughout the winter, insulated by their thick body feathers and feathered legs. The male sends out a deep drumming sound that resonates throughout the forest as he declares his territory by inflating his neck sacs. After mating, the female builds her nest in a depression in the ground under trees and shrubs and lines it with grasses, leaves, and feathers. She lays up to 10 pinkish, brown-spotted eggs that hatch in June to July.

Roger Rosenberger

Sooty Grouse

Heading through Hillside Flowers

As you begin your hike in June or July, you'll be on a hillside covered with the golden flowers of Mule's Ears (*Wyethia mollis*). Native Americans ate their seeds, and their flower stems were consumed as a vegetable. Their roots were mashed and applied to reduce swellings. Spurred Lupine (*Lupinus argenteus* var. *heteranthus*) grows among the Mule's Ears. These lupines form hairy, green seedpods that turn brown and become tightly twisted when the seeds are mature and ready to be expelled. I once had a basket of lupine pods on my desk that had been there awhile. One

Mule's Ears and Spurred Lupine

evening, I heard a loud pop, pop, pop coming from my office. When I entered the room to see what was up, I learned that lupines expel their seeds. I found them scattered all over the desk and floor and carried them outside, so they'd have a chance to germinate.

In this first part of the trail in July, you'll also find a spring-fed garden with the 5' tall plants and white, large flower clusters of the Corn Lily (*Veratrum californicum*). It's named for its flowers in bud, because they resemble corn kernels on a cob. The flower petals and sepals are identical, as is typical of the Lily Family. When it first rises out of the soil in spring, the leaves sheath the large, sturdy stems, so some people confuse it with the Skunk Cabbage, which doesn't grow at Tahoe. John Muir described it as "a plant determined to be seen." The entire plant is toxic and if consumed can slow down a person's heartbeat and even cause death. Because of its poison, the dried roots can be used as a natural insecticide. See p. 99.

Plainleaf Fawn Lily

In wet habitats, you'll find the **Plainleaf Fawn Lily**. It makes my heart sing, because it heralds the beginning of spring at Tahoe as it blooms by melting snow banks. It resembles the lower elevation Sierra Fawn Lily, which has spotted leaves, like spots on a fawn, but our high elevation lily lacks the spots, so it's called "Plainleaf." Its identical petals and sepals are white and yellow. After fertilization, the petals turn pink to purple and then fall off to reveal a three-sectioned ovary. If you view the ovary with the sun shining through it, you'll see rows of seeds neatly lined up in each translucent chamber. Though it annually produces seed, the Fawn Lily is a perennial with a bulb tucked away all winter under deep snow. In spring, the nutrients that have been stored in the bulb support its new growth.

Flowers In Dry Habitats

In June, as you wind your way down the slopes under Red Firs, Lodgepole Pines, and Jeffrey Pines, you're likely to find fabulous displays of the early blooming **Spreading Phlox**. Kneel down to inhale its fragrance and to see tiny anthers peeking out from the white or

Spreading Phlox

lavender flowers. Nearby, ground-covering plants of Davis' Knotweed (*Polygonum davisiae*) emerge in early spring with bright red stems and leaves. Red pigments absorb heat readily, which supports new growth. In the fall after the leaves stop photosynthesizing, their red pigment is revealed and covers the hillsides red again.

Davis' Knotweed

On slopes among the rocks, you'll see the shrubs of Huckleberry Oak and Pinemat Manzanita near the bright yellow blossoms of Wall Flowers and Sulphur Flowers. The **Single-stem Butterweed** is easy to identify, because its narrow, daisy-like flowers bloom on hairy, solitary stems that are usually a foot or more tall. "Senecio," is from Latin "senex" for "old man," which is a reference to the white, hairy pappus that surrounds each seed after they have matured.

Another yellow flower in this dry habitat is the California Wavewing (*Cymopterus terebinthinus*), which grows 6–12″ tall with dark green leaves divided into numerous tiny segments. Its yellow flowers grow at the tips of stems that radiate outward in varying lengths from a central point. Its leaves smell like celery, and its common name is for its flattened fruits that are winged with wavy edges.

Single-stem Butterweed

Arriving at Sanford Lake

Soon the trail crosses a creek and heads down through gardens of Crimson Columbines, Wandering Daisies, Scarlet Gilias, and White-veined Mallows. As the trail becomes steeper, you'll see views of the lake through the trees, and in dry, rocky areas, you'll find Azure Penstemon, pink Mountain Pride, and the

California Wavewing

Mountain Jewelflower

Douglas' Catchfly

Labrador Tea

Mountain Jewelflower. Its 4 small white to yellow or purple petals are curled and veined in purple. A purple or yellow, inflated calyx surrounds the petals. This flower doesn't seem like a jewel, until it's viewed through a hand lens. It grows from 4–12" tall with green to yellow leaves that surround the stem, which inspired its other name, "Shield-leaf." Nearby you'll find Douglas' Catchfly (*Silene douglasii*) with inflated, fused sepals and white flowers with lobed petals. Two white, petal-like appendages lie at the base of each petal.

When you reach Sanford Lake, leave the trail and walk to your right through pink mallows, red gilias, and lavender pennyroyals to the shoreline. You may be ready for a swim in this warmer than normal high-elevation lake. One afternoon, as I sat at the lake's edge with friends, an amazing thing happened. A tall swirl of water about 50' tall, formed like a small tornado, suddenly rose upward from the lake's surface. It moved rapidly across the water and then scooted up onto the land and suddenly dissipated. We were speechless! I've never seen anything like it again.

At the lake, you probably won't see a tornado, but you'll see the low growing shrubs of Labrador Tea with white, fuzzy-looking flowers and the taller shrubs of Creek Dogwoods, willows, and alders. You might even see a White-crowned Sparrow hiding in the shrubs and hear the male's sweet song. The female builds a nest on the ground or several feet above in dense shrubs. She builds her nest from bits of bark and other materials and then lines it with grass for her little treasures. The eggs are a pale bluish green with brown spots and are incubated and cared for by the females only.

White-crowned Sparrow

Walking to the Lake's Outlet

After enjoying this part of the lake, take the trail clockwise around the lake through the wet gardens of Alpine Lilies, Seep-spring Monkeyflowers, and Crimson Columbines. In a dense conifer forest, the trail passes through carpets of the low growing **Sierra Bilberry** with tiny, pink, urn-shaped flowers that hang downward. If you're lucky, you might be able to taste its small blue berries in September or October, unless the mice and other animals have gotten there first.

Sierra Bilberry

The Mountain Ash (*Sorbus californica*) is a shrub that grows up to 12' tall along the lake's edge under the conifers. Its leaves are pinnate with toothed leaflets, and its white flowers grow in clusters with fuzzy-looking, protruding stamens. During fall's crisp days, the leaves turn gorgeous shades of pink, yellow, and red. Its bright red berries feed bears and other animals.

Mountain Ash

Soon, you'll reach a flat campsite in the trees near the lake's shoreline. You may see Damselflies with the great name, "Vivid Dancer" that fly and flit above the water with iridescent blue and black striped bodies. The Nevada legislature made the Dancer its official state insect in 2009, after a contest was offered to elementary school children in the state to choose their favorite insects. Damselflies are related to Dragonflies, but Damselflies

Mountain Ash

male, not "at rest"!

brown female

Vivid Dancers mating, female below

are thinner, smaller, and usually hold their wings together vertically above their bodies at rest. Dragonflies differ by usually holding their wings horizontally at rest. The male Dancer is always blue, while the female is either identical or tan to gray. The male is protective of his territory, but when a female enters it, he grabs her to mate as they fly in tandem. Damselflies live for about 4–12 months as nymphs in the mud of ponds and slow moving streams. They are also often seen clinging to rocks and grasses as they hunt for aquatic insects. During this time, they pass through as many as twelve body changes, before they become adults. As adults, they have 3 thread-like structures that extend from the ends of their abdomens. These are their gills, which absorb oxygen from the water. After mating, the male holds the female as she deposits her eggs on vegetation under the water. The terrestrial adults we seeing flying over the water live for only a few days to a few weeks. See p. 99.

From the campsite area, you can wander toward the outlet creek on the east edge of the lake. As you walk across large, flat, granitic slabs, you'll

Star-flowered False Solomon's Seal

have fabulous mountain vistas and other views down into Downey Lake and other smaller lakes. If you continue around the lake to its outlet creek, you may find the small flowers of **Star-flowered False Solomon's Seal** blooming in July. Its white flowers grow with identical petals and sepals on plants that are 12″ or taller with parallel veined leaves that clasp the stems. Its prominent, white pistil is topped with a white stigma that glistens receptively in the sunlight. The flower's bright yellow anthers are hinged on the top of fleshy filaments. If you look closely at the stigma tips, can you tell if they've been dusted with yellow pollen? On those with pollen, you might just notice a rosy glow emanating from the flower's face as its fruits ripen into purple to black berries.

The similar and more common Western False Solomon's Seal (*Maianthemum racemosum*) grows with tiny, white to creamy flowers that grow in a tightly clustered group. Their common name refers to the shape of their leaves, which resemble those of the eastern Solomon's seal. The eastern plant is marked with round scars on its thick root, left by the leaf stems, after they have withered and fallen off in winter. The scars resemble the seal of King Solomon who ruled Israel in late 900 B.C. He was famous for his wisdom and fair treatment of "his" people. His kingly seal, two interlaced triangles, eventually came to represent ultimate wisdom and the mystic union of body and soul.

Western False Solomon's Seal

If you plan to spend the night by the lake under the stars, you may feel a mystic union with all of Nature. If you return home at the end of the day,

Vista from lake

Sanford Lake in the fall

Bilberry leaves in fall

I hope you'll feel the same mystic union, along with the exhilaration of spending the day by the sparkling waters of Sanford Lake. If you come here in the fall, you'll experience stunning color displays as the leaves turn red on the Bilberries and red to gold on the shrubs around the lake.

#2 Carr Lake to Island & Penner Lakes

Island Lake

 to

One Way: 3 miles
Trail Begins/Ends: 6,600'/7,100'
Map: NG: Tahoe National Forest, Sierra Buttes/Donner Pass
Wildflower Season: mid May through August

Island and Penner Lakes are reached on a moderate trail in the stunning backcountry of the Grouse Ridge area. Bright flowers cover the rocky flanks of Fall Creek Mountain by Island Lake before the trail meanders through shaded, woodland gardens of lush ferns and flowers on the way to Penner Lake. After an uphill climb on switchbacks, the trail crests a ridgeline and then heads down to a rock-strewn hillside perch, with distant views of Lake Culbertson and Lindsey Lake, while Penner Lake sits below nestled in the trees. Sunsets turn the waters of both Island and Penner Lake into satiny pink to golden as the sun slowly descends behind the mountains.

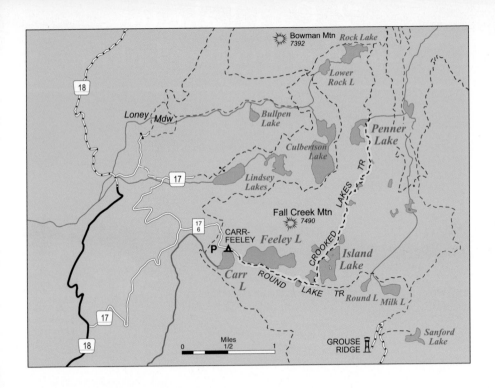

Featured Flowers

Kelloggia (*Kelloggia galioides*)
Large-flowered Collomia (*Collomia grandiflora*)
Slender Navarretia (*Navarretia leptalea*)
Yellow Pond-lily (*Nuphar polysepala*)
Labrador Tea (*Ledum glandulosum*)
Alpine Lily (*Lilium parvum*)

Trailhead Directions: **Driving west from Donner Summit or east from Colfax** on Highway 80. Take the Highway 20 exit and drive west on Highway 20 for 4.5 miles. Turn right onto Bowman Lake Road by the wooden shacks. **From Nevada City** at the intersection of Highways 20 and 49, head east on Highway 20 for 25.5 miles and turn left at Bowman Lake Road by the shacks. The turnoff is after the large, unsigned Bear Valley. Drive 8.4 miles along paved Bowman Lake Road (FR #18) to the Carr-Feeley Lake turnoff onto Grouse Ridge Road (FR #17) and drive 2.8 miles to the Carr Lake turnoff, up to the parking area. Arrive early on weekends and avoid the July 4th holiday. High clearance cars recommended. The NG map above covers up Island Lake with a label 12E11 and mislabels a small pond as Island Lake, but the trail to both lakes is easy to follow.

The trail begins on an old dirt road at a gate by the Carr-Feeley Trailhead sign and soon passes walk-in campsites by Carr Lake. (Contact PG & E at recinfo@pge.com). The tiny, pink flowers of **Kelloggia** bloom in early July through August as the hike begins. They are cute flowers that perch on fuzzy ovaries above 6–18″ tall stems and are 4-petaled or 5-petaled, which is unusual. Normally plants that have 5 petals don't also have flowers with 4 petals and visa versa. "Kelloggia" honors botanist, plant illustrator, and physician Dr. Albert Kellogg (1813–1887) who gathered plants at Tahoe, while botanizing from South to North America. He was a gentle, unassuming man with an inquisitive mind who loved nature. He was way ahead of his time, for he encouraged women to enter the sciences in the mid 1800s, when women were not admitted into universities. They were also considered too delicate to study botany, because flowers reproduce sexually.

Kelloggia

Other small flowers grow along the road, like the Spanish Lotus (*Acmispon americanus*), a "happy little traveler" found from Canada to Mexico. Its flower's banner petal is pink and its 2 wing petals are white and hide the reproductive parts in a keel, a shape formed by 2 fused petals. See p. 11. The Miniature Lotus (*Acmispon parviflorus*) has even tinier, pink to white pea flowers, and its leaves are both irregularly palmate and pinnate. Its flat, narrow, dark brown pods are shiny and up to 2½″ long.

Spanish Lotus

As you head uphill, there will be shrubs of Huckleberry Oak, Tobacco Brush, Whitethorn, and the 6–10′ tall Bittercherry (*Prunus imarginata*), which blooms in June with fuzzy-looking clusters of small, white flowers. Its serrated leaves are folded along the mid-vein, and they turn bright yellow in the fall. Its fruit is bitter for humans, but birds relish it. Native Americans used its bark for basketry and chewed the roots to treat canker sores.

Miniature Lotus

Bitter Cherry

Large-flowered Collomia

In damp, grassy areas look for the **Large-flowered Collomia** that grows up to about 2½′ tall. Its flowers are in tight groups with long tubes rising up to their pale, salmon-orange petals with blue anthers. It isn't a large flower, but it is much larger than Tahoe's other Collomia species.

Nearby, look for the **Slender Navarretia** that blooms in delicate masses with lavender pink petals and blue anthers. Find its fuzzy, white anthers in several flowers. Do some flowers have anthers with a red dot in the middle of them? Do other anther clusters have a red thread in the middle or a red thread with delicate lobes that resemble a tiny flower? What do you think is happening? See mallows on p. 177.

When you arrive at a creek that crosses a side trail off the road, don't head to the left on the road, which crosses over the dam. Instead head straight over the creek and directly up to the dam on Feeley Lake to pick up the Round Lake Trail. Fall Creek Mountain looms above the lake and in late May or June, under the Red Firs, you'll find the pretty, white petaled flowers of the Plainleaf Fawn Lily. Later in June, Wandering Daisies begin blooming alongside various lupines, paintbrushes, and gilias. In June after reaching a tiny meadow on your left, you'll find pink Alpine Shooting Stars, yellow Plantain Buttercups, and yellow Primrose Monkeyflowers as the trail starts climbing more steeply.

Slender Navarretia

closed stigma   *open stigma*

A Lily Pond with River Otters

Near the top of the climb, the trail veers left until a small pond on the right comes into view. In the pond, you'll see the flowers of the **Yellow Pond-lily** blooming early July through August. Its young leaves coil beneath the water, but as they mature they uncoil and float, forming a peaceful resting place for little frogs. The disk-shaped stigma is in the flower's center and is surrounded by downward curving stamens. Its seeds mature in the fall and are a rich source of food for waterfowl. They were gathered from California to Montana by Native Americans and were parched and then ground into a flour. The Klamath people of southern Oregon collected the seedpods by boat and roasted them to make

Yellow Pond-lily

a kind of popcorn-tasting meal. The rootstocks cling to the soil on the pond's bottom and were eaten by the Washoe people in soups and stews. The roots are a favored food of waterfowl also.

While you're at the pond, find a hiding place by the trees to sit quietly. River Otters are found in ponds and rivers and can often be seen here on the pond's grassy island or you may see them swimming swiftly through the water as they hunt for fish or frogs. Otters are playful mammals that live in waterside burrows or dens. They dig tunnels from their dens to move safely to the water, and since they are active all winter, they

River Otter

find ice holes in the pond's surface through which they breathe. The females live in groups with other females and deliver their 1–6 pups in an underground den. The mother raises her pups on her own and after about 2 months, she guides her young into the water, and they quickly learn to swim.

As the trail continues, it crosses the pond's outlet creek and follows the edge of the pond past the ground-carpeting Sierra Bilberry (*Vaccinium caespitosum*) with its tiny pink flowers, and Macloskey's Violet (*Viola macloskeyi*) with small white flowers. On the hill above the trail, the 18″ tall Slender Penstemon (*Penstemon gracilentus*) grows with narrow, tubular, blue flowers. You'll also find the 12–18″ tall Pine Lupine (*Lupinus albicaulis*) that blooms with

Pine Lupine

Labrador Tea by Fall Creek Mountain

purple and white flowers above palmate leaves divided into 5–10 leaflets. Its flowers turn brown after pollination and remain on the stem along with the fresh flowers.

Soon the trail climbs uphill through the Red Fir forest until it arrives at a pond on the left, backdropped by Fall Creek Mountain where you'll find the evergreen shrubs of **Labrador Tea**. Their white flowers grow in clusters with dark green, leathery leaves that are glandular-hairy beneath. Indigenous people knew how to safely brew the leaves into a medicinal tea, but some sources warn that "ledo," a toxic substance in the leaves, can be poisonous in large amounts and cause paralysis or even death.

Approaching Island Lake

Just beyond the pond at the trail fork, take the Crooked Lakes Trail toward Penner Lake. Soon, you'll pass another smaller pond where in June or early July you'll find the 1' tall shrubs of Mountain Heather (*Phyllodoce breweri*). Its pinkish red flowers grow in clusters with leaves that are needle-like. Nearby will be the 3' tall Mountain Spiraea (*Spiraea splendens*) with tiny, very fragrant flowers that enclose numerous extended stamens that make the blossoms look fuzzy. Its leaves are serrated along the upper edges, as is typical in the Rose Family.

As the trail climbs over rock slabs, you'll pass white and lavender mats of fragrant Spreading Phlox and the white, urn-shaped, drooping flowers of Pinemat Manzanita. At this point, you'll be 1.2 miles from the trailhead as Island Lake comes into view. Unless you're planning to veer right at the lake to find the best campsites among the trees, head left and follow the trail along the lake's left side, until you arrive at a peninsula that extends into the lake. As you walk out on top of the peninsula, look to your left at the first island with its rock slabs, where you may see playful otters sliding down into the lake.

Pinemat Manzanita

Yellow Sulphur Flower and pink Mountain Pride bloom on the peninsula in July. In August to September Wright's Buckwheat (*Eriogonum wrightii*) blooms in low clumps with tiny, white, red-striped, petal-like sepals. Buck-

Wright's Buckwheat

wheats lack petals and instead attract insects with their colored sepals. The leaves and stems are densely covered with white hairs to reflect sunlight and to reduce evaporation. Island Lake has comfortable temperatures for summer swimming, but please don't swim to the otter's island and disturb them. Let's leave that island as their playground. Instead, take your swim from the tip of the peninsula to the other island.

Wright's Buckwheat flowers

Walking up Fall Creek Mountain

Island Lake's peninsula sits at the flank of Fall Creek Mountain. Hiking up to its 7,490' summit will take you past hillsides of flowers in June and July. Since there is no trail, you'll be following the ridgeline and creating your own path through the plants, responding to the flowers that beckon

Sulphur Flowers and Azure Penstemons on Fall Creek Mountain

Alpine Lilies

*White-flowered
Bog Orchids*

you. When you reach the top after a final rock-scramble, you'll have lovely, distant vistas. After leaving the mountain and returning to the trail, continue heading north through lush, forested habitats of ferns, white orchids, red paintbrushes, and beautiful displays of the **Alpine Lily**. It grows 5–6′ tall with orange, identical petals and sepals. The flowers are marked with spots to attract pollinators, and its large leaves whorl around the stems. You'll also find the White-flowered Bog Orchid (*Platanthera leucostachys*) with tiny flowers that grow along stems up to 2½′ tall. Insects are attracted by the flower's fragrance and nectar. After the flowers are pollinated, the seeds mature in capsules that open to release their little treasures to be dispersed by the wind.

Continuing along the trail, you'll pass a junction with the Crooked Lakes trail. Veer left there past views of Black Buttes in the distance onto a final 0.5-mile climb up switchbacks to a ridgeline. Sulphur Flower, Jewelflower, Azure Penstemon, and Woolly Sunflower grow on the hillsides. Shrubs of Cream Bush (*Holodiscus discolor*), up to about 4′ tall, live among the rocks with gold-centered, creamy white blossoms, and leaves that are deeply veined and velvety soft.

After the switchbacks, you'll arrive at the ridgeline, and as you descend, you'll catch a glimpse of Penner

Lake in the trees below. As you continue on the trail toward the lake, a short spur on the left leads to a rocky hillside above the lake with wildflowers growing among the rocks. You'll see Penner Lake in the trees below and look out toward Culbertson and Lindsey Lakes in the distance.

Cream Bush

Arriving at Penner Lake

After enjoying the rock garden flowers, return to the main trail and head left to continue down to 7,100' Penner Lake. The pleasure of this lake is its remote and wild feeling compared to popular Island Lake. Island Lake is a short walk in and is such a scenic lake that most people stop there. So Penner Lake is usually more peaceful with fewer people. It also has nice campsites and cozy lakeside picnic spots.

Wavy-leaved Paintbrush and Nuttal's Larkspur

It's a short, grassy walk by conifers and Mountain Spiraea (*Spiraea splendens*) along the lake, with many places to stop for wildflowers. The remote feeling here nourishes my need for wildness, which for me means a deep sense of connection with Nature and the freedom to wander at will through a beautiful setting that makes my soul sing and fills my heart with joy. Thoreau once wrote, "Our life would stagnate if it were not for the unexplored forests and meadows which surround it. We need the tonic of wilderness. We can never have enough of it."

Spurred Lupine and Mule's Ears

Even though this area is no longer "unexplored," we can still feel the "tonic of wilderness" at Penner Lake. Whether you're here to wander among

Penner Lake

the rocks for the summer wildflowers and flowers at the lake's edge or come later for the red berries and golden colors of fall, this special lake will nurture you with its powerful energy and peace.

After leaving Penner Lake, it's a special experience to return to the peninsula on Island Lake for an early evening picnic dinner to watch the full moon rise over the lake. The peninsula is the best place to do this, because without trees and on a clear night, the moon will light up the rocks like a giant floodlight. Hiking out from the peninsula under the full moon is a very different experience from day hiking. A headlamp helps in the deep darkness of the trees, but I only turn it on when necessary. Instead, I allow my eyes to adjust to the darkness and then slowly begin walking along the trail, feeling my way, sensing with my feet, using the moonlight to guide me. At night, I become more intensely aware of the power of trees as their darkened forms stand out against the moonlight. I'm even more sensitive to the fragrances, changing temperatures, and night sounds. A sweet comfort at night is the gentle "hooting" of a screech owl, which sounds like a little ball softly bouncing down a hill. In the darkness, all my senses come alive, awakened in a different way as I surrender to the mountain, walking slowly . . . sensing the trail without seeing it, and so discover myself to be the animal that I truly am, who also belongs here on this evening . . . under this moon.

#3 Loney Meadow Loop

Loney Meadow Penstemons

One-mile level loop
Trail elevation: 6,000′
Map: NG: Tahoe National Forest, Sierra Buttes/Donner Pass
Wildflower Season: May to August

Loney is a beautiful high country meadow, which begins blooming soon after the snows melt, with flowers that form a changing tapestry of color as the summer unfolds. Those who love Violets will be delighted with the meadow's five species. Loney is fun for youngsters, because the trail around the meadow is both short and level, and all can enjoy the meadow for its many bird species. In fall, the Aspens turn yellow, and autumn colored grasses move in the late afternoon breezes like waves rolling across an ocean.

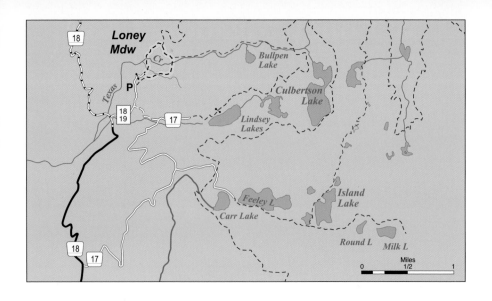

Featured Flowers

Primrose Monkeyflower (*Mimulus primuloides*)
Meadow Penstemon (*Penstemon rydbergii*)
Bleeding Heart (*Dicentra formosa*)
Fan Violet (*Viola sheltonii*)
Long-spurred Violet (*Viola adunca*)
Blue-eyed Grass (*Sisyrinchium idahoense*)

Trailhead Directions: **Driving west from Donner Summit or east from Colfax** on Highway 80. Take the Highway 20 exit and drive west on Highway 20 for 4.5 miles. Turn right onto Bowman Lake Road by the wooden shacks. **From Nevada City** at the intersection of Highways 20 and 49, head east on Highway 20 for 25.5 miles and turn left at Bowman Lake Road by the shacks. The turnoff is after the large, unsigned Bear Valley.

Continue driving along blacktopped Bowman Lake Road until it turns to dirt. At 10.4 miles, you'll pass the Loney Meadow sign and at 10.5 miles, turn right by the funky Lindsey Creek sign. Drive up the short hill and take a left at the split to avoid the steep road. After a short uphill, you'll arrive at an old shack and a meadow of Pussy Paws that color a small meadow pink in June. Veer to the right and then left to continue driving another 0.3 mile (don't take side roads to the right), until you reach a road on the left that lacks a sign indicating it is the road to Loney Meadow. Turn left and drive 0.4 mile to the trailhead parking. High-clearance cars are recommended.

The trail begins on the road by the locked metal gate and soon turns into a trail that continues along the meadow's west side of the loop trail; we'll return on east side of the loop. Near the gate, you'll see a small meadow in the trees off to your left that is fun to visit in June for its special flowers. The white Macloskey's Violet blooms here by the yellow flowers of **Primrose Monkeyflower**. Each small flower is on a solitary stem above its basal, hairy leaves. In early morning, if there are dewdrops on its leaves and if the sun angle is just right, the sunlight forms a prism or spectrum of light like a rainbow in the tiny dewdrops on the leaves. The Thyme-leaved Veronica (*Veronica serpyllifolia*) also grows there with a demure, little flower that has blue flowers veined in a dark blue. Its two stamens extend outward topped with blue anthers. A white style rises above the green ovary and is topped with a rounded, bumpy stigma.

Return to the road and veer left past the gate toward Loney Meadow. When you are in view of the meadow, you'll find a Red and White Fir next to each other, which will give you a chance to compare their needles. See p. 19. Under the firs in late May and June, you'll find the white flowers of the Plainleaf Fawn Lily and the 3–4' tall shrubs of the Sierran Gooseberry (*Ribes roezlii*). Its small flowers hang down along the branches, and its dark red sepals are curled backward and fused into a red, hairy tube. The small, red and white tipped flower encloses dark anthers and yellow styles with a tiny, dark stigma. Its spiny fruit makes a delicious jelly, after cooking to break down the spines. The fruit of various Ribes species are rich in vitamins and minerals and were eaten by Native Americans throughout California.

Primrose Monkeyflowers

Dewdrops on the Monkeyflower leaves

Thyme-leaved Veronica

Sierran Gooseberry (left) and Gooseberry fruit (right)

Blue-eyed Mary

Blue-eyed Mary

Seep-spring Monkey flower

Nevada Lewisia

Indigenous People and Meadow Wildflowers

As the trail enters the wide-open meadow, I pause to remember the indigenous people who came to Loney Meadow for thousands of years to hunt and trade. They must have appreciated this meadow as they dug up the camas lily bulbs and gathered buttercup seeds to roast. Much later, in the 1800s, the Loney family grazed cattle in the meadow and built a dairy facility to provide milk for the local foothill communities.

Tiny, ¼" wide, blue and white flowers bloom near the trail on stems 1–16" tall. These Blue-eyed Mary flowers (*Collinsia parviflora*) are so tiny you'll need to look at them with a hand lens to appreciate their sweet beauty. Soon the trail crosses a small bridge over a tributary and then crosses a second bridge over Texas Creek with Seep-spring Monkey flowers along the creek's edges. After a good snow year, the flowers in the meadow create a vast, changing sea of color. Quamash Camas Lilies, yellow buttercups, and pink shooting stars begin blooming in mid May and are soon followed by purple penstemons, pink bog mallows, red paintbrushes, and blue to purple lupines.

Look also in the grasses for the 1" wide, white to pale pink flowers of the Nevada Lewisia (*Lewisia nevadensis*). It grows 1–3" tall with fleshy leaves that radiate outward below the flowers. Each flower has 5–10 petals but only 2 sepals. Native Americans removed the outer skin of the roots and consumed the roots after they were boiled to remove their bitterness.

The most intense flower show in the meadow, after the camas lilies and buttercups, is created by **Meadow Penstemons**, which in a good snow year create a sea of blue purple flowers. This is our only wet meadow penstemon. Its glabrous, tubular flowers

Meadow Penstemon

have two upper petals and three lower ones, and the flowers grow in whorls around the upper part of its 8–20″ tall stems. Its staminode is densely hairy. See p. 125.

Woodland Flowers

The Tuberous Sanicle (*Sanicula tuberosa*) grows in sunny areas among the conifers on reddish stems up to 8″ tall with tiny clusters of yellow umbel flowers. On a warm day, the Sanicles emit a strong cilantro-like fragrance. Their flowers are either staminate (with stamens only) or bisexual (with pistils and stamens). The staminate flowers have tiny flower stems, and the bisexual flowers lack stems. An elegant flower, the **Bleeding Heart**, grows at elevations under 7,000′, so you won't see it in many places at Tahoe. It blooms on stems up to about 12″ tall above finely divided leaves. Its name comes from its pink, heart-shaped flowers that seem to "bleed" from the base.

Tuberous Sanicle

Gardens of Violets

In June and July in a good snow year, five species of violets grow in the meadow. Violets are identified by their 5 petals and single nectar spur. The pistil is in the throat of the spur and is surrounded by 5 stamens. The two lower stamens project into the spur to form drops of nectar. Bees, moths, and butterflies pollinate violets with a flexible proboscis that reaches down the spur to sip the nectar. Their seeds develop in a little canoe-shaped structure, and when they mature, the sides of the "canoe" squeeze together to pop the seeds out onto the ground.

Bleeding Heart

In damp, mossy gardens look for the white flowers of Macloskey's Violet (*Viola macloskeyi*). Its lower petal is marked with purple nectar lines, and the lateral petals have slight markings and tiny white hairs that gather pollen from visiting insects.

Macloskey's Violet

Fan Violet

Stream Violet

Mountain Violet

Long-spurred Violet

The yellow flowered **Fan Violet** grows in damp woodland gardens, with fan-shaped leaves that are deeply lobed. Stream Violet (*V. glabella*) blooms yellow in very wet gardens with the typical heart-shaped leaves. Its 2–3″ long naked stems support the flowers well above the leaves. The yellow Mountain Violet (*V. purpurea*) lives in sunny, drying habitats. Its upper petals are dark purple to brownish on the back, and the lateral petals are also often colored the same.

The purple flowers of **Long-spurred Violet** are found in wet areas. It is easy to identify by its spur. The two lateral petals are fuzzy with white hairs that gather the pollen from insects. Its typical violet leaves remind me of the violets that I loved as a child in my garden. If you kneel down to look at all the different violets here, you'll feel more appreciation for their beauty. Georgia O'Keeffe once said, ". . . nobody sees a flower, really, it is so small . . . we haven't time . . . and to see takes time, like to have a friend takes time."

A Violet That Never Blooms

If you hike the trail later in summer, you may find green, cleistogamous flowers as buds hidden in the leaves of the Mountain and Fan Violets. "Cleistogamous" is from Greek for "closed marriage." Violets bloom early in spring, when freezing temperatures can damage their reproductive parts and when pollinators are few. In response, some violets have evolved two different kinds of flowers: a

Violet seeds

colorful one that blooms early in the season and a later-forming flower bud that never opens. Instead, it self-pollinates when its reproductive parts mature and touch to produce clones of the mother plant as a backup in case the early flower isn't pollinated.

Cleistogamy is unusual, because most plants have processes or mechanisms to avoid self-pollination. Cross-pollination provides more options for adapting to changing environments or to other stresses. In the exciting field of epigenetics, scientists are learning that plants can adapt more quickly than was formerly realized, not only by a process of slow evolution but by turning their genes off or on. This is a simplification, but the book *Spontaneous Evolution*, by Bruce H. Lipton, Ph.D. and Steve Bhaerman, offers a scientifically fascinating and enjoyable discussion of this subject.

Blue-eyed Grass (Sisyrinchium idahoense)

Boggy Environment Plants

The showiest plant in the boggy meadow is the white flowered, 5–6' tall Corn Lily (*Veratrum californicum*). The Iris called **Blue-eyed Grass** grows near-by. Irises aren't grasses but are named for their grass-like leaves. "Sisyrinchium" is the ancient Greek name. Its leafless stems are up to 2' tall. Their flowers have identical blue sepals and petals that are marked with dark nectar lines, yellow throats, and yellow anthers. Tucked down in the grasses are the tiny treasures of the 5-petaled, ¼" flowers of Chickweed (*Stellaria media*), which are lobed so deeply, they appear to have 10 petals. Their bright red anthers fade to brown after their pollen is released. The Swamp Onion (*Allium validum*) is at home in boggy areas right next to the Chickweeds and blooms with round clusters of pink flowers. Its flowers sit atop 4' solitary, leafless stems.

Chickweed

Chickweed flower

Swamp Onion

Quaking Aspens

Quaking Aspens (*Populus tremuloides*) grow along the edges of the wet meadow and are one of Tahoe's most beloved trees for their fluttering leaves and yellow to orange fall color. Their flat leaves are attached 90 degrees to the flattened leaf stems, which causes them to "dance with delight" in the tiniest of breezes. Aspens are unusual, because they carry out photosynthesis in the green tissue beneath their white bark. This allows them to begin photosynthesizing early in the season, before they leaf out.

Aspen seeds don't successfully germinate in the arid forests of the west, so they primarily reproduce by sprouting from spreading roots to form large groves of clones, which are genetically identical trees. Individual aspens live for about 150 years or so before they die, but the cloned group is a single organism that lives much longer. According to the US Forest Service, "The largest and oldest known aspen clone is the 'Pando' clone on the Fishlake National Forest in southern Utah. It is over 100 acres in size . . . It has been aged at 80,000 years, although 5–10,000 year-old clones are more common."

Red-breasted Sapsucker

Loney Meadow Birds and a Surprise

A number of birds are found in the meadow, including Warblers, Black-headed Grosbeaks, Western Tanagers, Mountain Bluebirds, and even the fabulous Pileated Woodpecker. The Red-breasted Sapsucker is common and feeds on the sap and cambium of aspens and cottonwoods. They drill horizontal holes into the trunks and branches and use a brush-like tongue to sip the sap as it flows out. They also consume insects caught in the sap or catch them in flight. Their young are raised in nests in cavities of large aspens, and after a week or so of leaving the nest, their parents have taught them how drill their own little holes in small willows.

The trail soon crosses Texas Creek and then heads into a boggy area of the meadow where in June you'll find large carpets of Plantain Buttercups (*Ranunculus alismifolius*). Their yellow flowers grow above 2–6″ long leaves that are narrow, glabrous, and smooth-edged. The Western Buttercup (*Ranunculus occidentalis*) is found in dryer areas of the meadow, growing up to 2′ tall. Its leaves are hairy and deeply lobed and toothed. Buttercup seeds sit in clusters. Each seed is flattened and topped with a tiny beak. They were gathered by Native Americans and roasted in flat, tightly woven baskets with hot coals to parch out their toxins. After cooking, the seeds tasted like popcorn and were added to other foods or stored in little baskets to be passed out to family and friends as a delicacy.

Plantain Buttercups

The walk through the grasses on this side of the meadow will take you along the creek. One day as I was walking through the meadow, thinking I had seen just about everything that day, a pair of Sandhill Cranes came swooping down to feed by the creek. I watched them for a long time, thrilled to be sharing the meadow with these large, prehistoric-like birds, which are more commonly found in the Sacramento Valley. After walking through the meadow along the creek, you can pick up the trail and enjoy more flowers as you return to your car.

Western Buttercup and flower

Western Buttercup seeds

#4 Loch Leven Lakes

Lower Loch Leven Lake

👟 👟 👟 👟

One Way: 3.8 miles to High Loch Leven Lake
Trail Begins/Ends: 5,680'/6,850'
Map: NG: Tahoe National Forest, Sierra Buttes/Donner Pass
Wildflower Season: late May to August

The popular Loch Leven Lakes Trail is a steady uphill climb that reaches a series of lakes scattered among the conifers, like a giant broken necklace whose beads have rolled away to find their own special niches. The hike to the lakes passes slopes of flowers in a variety of habitats. A wooden bridge crosses a creek that is fun for wading on a warm summer day. Beyond the bridge, yellow monkeyflowers and violets bloom in a secret seep garden beneath the shelter of alders. To the delight of adults and children, Buffleheads and Mallards with their ducklings can be seen swimming and playing in the lakes.

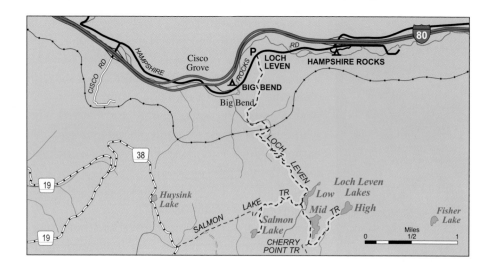

Featured Flowers

Spreading Dogbane (*Apocynum androsaemifolium*)

Azure Penstemon (*Penstemon azureus*)

Fendler's Meadow Rue (*Thalictrum fendleri*)

Torrey's Monkeyflower (*Mimulus torreyi*)

Brewer's Monkeyflower (*Mimulus breweri*)

Horsemint (*Agastache urticifolia*)

Trailhead Directions: **Heading west from Truckee** on Interstate 80 past Donner Summit, take the Rainbow Road exit. Turn left at the bottom of the off-ramp, drive under the freeway, and turn right onto Hampshire Rocks Road. **Heading east** on I-80, take the Rainbow Road exit, and from the exit ramp, turn right onto Hampshire Rocks Road. In 0.9 mile, you'll arrive at the trailhead parking. The highway noise fades away as the trail climbs higher.

The trail begins across from the parking lot by an old wooden sign and climbs along granitic slabs past shrubs of Pinemat Manzanita, Huckleberry Oak, and **Spreading Dogbane** that blooms in June and July below the shrubs with small, ¼″ long, white to pink flowers. The toxic, bitter, milky sap in the stems can cause skin blisters in some people and discourages browsing animals. The stem fibers of certain species of Dogbane were used by Native Americans

Spreading Dogbane

Azure Penstemon

to make twine and rope. You'll also find two of our most beautiful penstemons. Mountain Pride (*Penstemon newberryi*) blooms bright pink in rocky habitats and **Azure Penstemon** puts on a show all along the trail with yellow buds and blue to purplish flowers. Its lower petals are marked with white nectar lines to guide insects toward the anthers, which curl downward, enticing pollinators with their gifts of pollen.

A Flower with a "Hula Skirt"?

Soon the trail descends into a forest and then climbs uphill through more shrubs, until it descends again into a boggy area in the forest. There in shafts of sunlight, you'll find Bracken Ferns, Crimson Columbines, Arrowleaf Butterweeds, and the Alpine Lily (*Lilium parvum*), which grows up to 5' tall with orange, spotted, identical petals and sepals. The dioecious male and female plants of **Fendler's Meadow Rue** are nearby with nodding flowers that lack petals to attract pollinators, which is a clue that they are wind pollinated. The flowers of the male plants have green sepals that hang downward with pink filaments and yellow anthers,

Alpine Lily

which resemble tiny "hula skirts" when they dance in the wind. The female plants have green, star-shaped ovaries that swell as the ovules mature into seeds. Wander among them to see if you can find both the male and female

Meadow Rue, male

Meadow Rue, female

plants. They're sure to be there, because a Meadow Rue garden is a happy place where females eagerly await the attention of the neighboring males.

Mountain Violet

Arriving at the Wooden Bridge and Creek
As the trail heads uphill past large Junipers, it arrives at a slope with huge granite slabs. Here the trail becomes hard to follow, because there is no obvious trail over the solid granite slabs. Just continue uphill staying to the right. Look for "ducks" or cairns made up of three stacked rocks, which mark the way. At the top of the slabs, the dirt trail continues to the right through the trees to a pond, which can dry into a small meadow in late summer. Walk to the end of the pond and head straight along the poorly defined trail to more granite slabs and a sandy, rocky trail marked with "ducks." From there, the trail is easy to follow.

White to lavender flowers of Spreading Phlox (*Phlox diffusa*) flow lavishly over the rocks by shrubs of white Tobacco Bush, Serviceberry, and Whitethorn. The dry habitat Mountain Violet (*Viola purpurea*) blooms in the sandy soil with yellow flowers that are purplish brown on the backs of their upper petals. The leaves are green to grayish green and vary in shape. The Nodding Microseris (*Microseris nutans*) grows with flowers that nod in bud and become upright in flower. Their flowers are composed of small ray flowers only. The Nude Buckwheat (*Eriogonum nudum*) is found in the same habitat and is named for its naked (leafless) stems. Nude Buckwheat grows up to 3' tall with tight clusters of small flowers decorated with red anthers. It seems unimpressive from a distance, but its flowers are lovely and delicate when viewed through a hand lens.

Nodding Microseris

In less than a mile, you'll arrive at an alder-lined creek and wooden bridge. It's fun to explore the creek both above and below the bridge for

Nude Buckwheat and flower

Creek wading

California Mountain Ash

wading and for picnics on the boulder slabs by Mountain Alders and Creek Dogwoods. Mountain Ash (*Sorbus californica*) grows below the bridge with white flowers. Its bright red berries are bitter until the frost in fall sweetens them. It grows up to 12′ tall, with pinnate leaves that have seven to nine toothed leaflets.

When you arrive at sandy flats in open areas, look for small plants with pink flowers. One of these, **Torrey's Monkeyflower** grows up to about 3″ tall, with dainty flowers that sweetly look upward from their dry, barren habitat. The reproductive parts lie hidden within the flower tube, but if you gently part the petals, you can see their delicate beauty. Each little anther resembles a teensie, ruffly, white flower. The smaller **Brewer's Monkeyflower** grows in the same habitat, often carpeting the soil at the base of Jeffrey Pines. It's an annual about 4–6″ tall with pink flowers, marked with yellow and red spots. Its narrow leaves are glandular-hairy, and its fused sepals form a calyx that is glandular-hairy and ridged. If you spot this tiny flower, you have excellent eyes and a botanical sixth sense!

Torrey's Monkeyflower

Brewer's Monkeyflower

An Enchanted Garden

After crossing the wooden bridge, you'll enter a cool, lush understory garden with 15′ tall alders shading the path. When you arrive at a small, spring-fed creek across the trail, look among the leafy growth for an enchanting little garden of Stream Violets, Crimson Columbines, and Alpine Lilies. As you continue on, you'll see 4–5′ tall **Horsemints** with pinkish lavender to white flowers tucked in a rosy purple calyx. Four white stamens protrude from the flower with purple anthers. The plant's main stem is square, which is typical of the Mint family. Its triangular leaves have serrated edges and can be steeped for tea, though for me the flavor is too intense. Indigenous people drank the tea to induce sweating to heal colds. Monarch Butterflies and Western Tiger Swallowtails feed on its nectar.

Horsemint

In a little over a mile from the trailhead, you'll arrive at the railroad tracks of the original 1860s Central Pacific Railroad. It was built by Chinese laborers. Sadly, many of them died while working on it. Be extremely careful crossing the tracks; trains pass frequently through here and are very hard to hear, until they are dangerously close. After the tracks, you'll hike through a forest and then begin an 800′ climb for 1.5 miles on a series of tiring, rockstrewn switchbacks. Along the way, to catch your breath, look for the reddish Spotted Coralroot Orchid (*Corallorhiza maculata*) that grows under the conifers without leaves, but with white petals that are red spotted. Look also for the red Snow Plant (*Sarcodes sanguinea*) that resembles a 12–18″ tall, fat asparagus, which is startling in the forest duff.

Snow Plants

Arriving at Lower Loch Leven

After the trail levels out on a comfortable dirt path, it passes through an open forest and then arrives at a small summit with a view below of Lower Loch Leven Lake. From there you'll head down a steep rocky but short trail past Azure Penstemons and reach the lake. In June to early July, pink Mountain Heather, white Cassiope, and Labrador Tea bloom. Look also for more carpets of Spreading Phlox, pink tufts of Pussy Paws, and pink White-veined

Pussy Paws

Fireweed

Fireweed stigma

Mallows that bloom in profusion during most of the summer on the slope above the lake.

In late July, the pink satiny flowers of Fireweed bloom at the lake's edge on plants 4–5' or taller. Notice its inferior ovary, which is the long swelling below the petals. This is where the seeds will develop. When mature, the ovary dries and splits lengthwise to release its fluffy, tufted seeds that are spread by the wind. Notice that some stigmas are closed, while others are 4-lobed. The 4-lobed stigma is ready to receive pollen from another Fireweed, because its own pollen has been released, and its ovules are readly to be fertilized. If any of its blue pollen remains on the anthers, check it out with your hand lens. Native Americans ate its young spring shoots like asparagus, and its spring leaves were brewed for tea. Fireweed leaves are lovely in the fall, when they turn bright red.

Lower Loch Leven is warmer than most other Tahoe lakes, and its shoreline offers campsites and large granite slabs for warm sunbathing after a swim. In July, if you sit by the lake before walking on, you may see Bufflehead ducks playing in the water and Mallards followed by their ducklings. To continue on toward Middle Loch Leven Lake, head to the right along the lake past yellow floating Pond-lilies, and you'll shortly arrive at a junction

Salmon Lake junction

by a sign that doesn't mention Salmon Lake. If you want to check out Salmon Lake, head right at the junction for a few feet until you see a sign on your left up in a Jeffrey Pine. Continue on this trail for about 0.6 mile, and when the trail forks, take a left and continue for another 0.3 mile down to the lake.

It's usually very private and peaceful and is also pleasant for swimming. This lake is especially fun for children, when it is alive with busy iridescent blue, "Vivid Dancer" Damselflies flitting about in wild courtship, forming . . . can you believe it . . . a small heart as they unite.

Reaching the Higher Lakes

The main trail continues past the Salmon Lake junction for about 0.3 mile downhill and then up a short climb to gorgeous Middle Loch Leven Lake. This large lake is beautiful and very popular, but big enough to usually find a special spot to spend the day or to camp with some privacy.

Bright Mountain Heather blooms along its shores in June, and Spurred Lupines bloom on the dry slopes above the lake much of the summer. Nice campsites may entice you to stay, but if you want to continue on to High Loch Leven, take a walk around the lake's southern tip to reach a junction with the Cherry Point Trail sign. Go left at the sign and continue along a sometimes, confusing trail that is marked with faded blotches of orange paint that help to mark the trail

Trail to High Loch Leven

through the rocks. Along the way, the trail winds through groves of pink Mountain Spiraea and past glimpses of the blue waters of Middle Loch Leven. Soon, it enters a shady, damp, woodland garden, where the trail becomes a bit confusing. Take the short, steep, bouldered, orange-marked trail to your right, which heads up on a few boulders to a gradual, sunny trail that passes by a large cairn, marking the trail. Continue through more trees until the trail levels out at High Loch Leven Lake. The old lake sign has the elevation as 6,220′, but the USFS maps have it as 6,850′.

High Loch Leven lake

Lance-leaf Stonecrop

Spreading Phlox

This lovely alpine lake is back-dropped by rocky slopes and in June through August, you'll find Azure Penstemons, yellow Sulphur flowers and Woolly Sunflowers by red, Wavy-leaved Paintbrushes. Later in the season Explorer's Gentian blooms by the lake. You'll also find the tiny, white Bud Saxifrage, along with a myriad of other hues and shapes created from sedums, sandworts, phlox, and other treasures. Since it is the farthest lake from the trail-head, it's usually a peaceful place with good lakeside camping and swimming to spend serene days in close contact with nature. Days like this are the best, and remember . . . just loafing is honor-able work! Walt Whitman once wrote, "I lean and loaf at my ease, observing a spear of summer grass."

Leichtlin's Mariposa Lilies & Wavy-leaved Paintbrush

I've spent many days at Tahoe with no agenda, just loafing, enjoying the blue sky overhead, the fragrance of the trees, and the pleasure of a soft breeze caressing my face. When we are very still and curious about what surrounds us, we see more, and we lose all sense of time while sinking into the sweet bliss of the timeless, present moment.

#5 Mt. Judah & Donner Peak Loop

Sulphur Flowers on Mt. Judah

👟👟 – 👟👟👟👟

Loop: approximately 6 miles
One Way: 1.6 miles to Donner Peak only
Trail Begins/Ends: 7,120'/8,243'
Map: NG: Tahoe National Forest, Sierra Buttes/Donner Pass
Wildflower Season: June through September

The Mount Judah Loop follows the Pacific Crest Trail along the ridge of the Sierra with breathtaking views of distant mountain ranges while below, Donner Lake sparkles in the afternoon sunlight. Flowers on open slopes form yellow, pink, and purple swaths of undulating color on windy days, and vibrant primroses, rock fringes, and penstemons strut their stuff among the granite boulders. In August to September, fall blooming fuchsias, gentians, and rabbitbrush sparkle like jewels on the steep talus slopes.

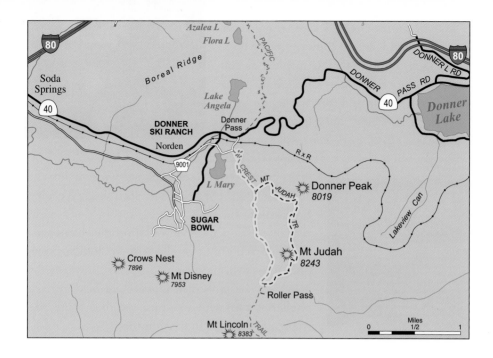

Featured Flowers

Western Snakeroot (*Ageratina occidentalis*)
Rosy Sedum (*Rhodiola integrifolia*)
Mountain Pennyroyal (*Monardella odoratissima*)
Rock Fringe (*Epilobium obcordatum*)
Potbelly Owl's Clover (*Orthocarpus cuspidatus subsp. cryptanthus*)
Brewer's Bishop's Cap (*Pectiantia breweri*)

Trailhead Directions: **Driving west** on Interstate-80 from Truckee, take the Donner Lake exit and drive left over the freeway to the stop sign. Drive through the intersection onto Donner Pass Road (Old Hwy 40) and then past the excellent Visitor's Center in Donner Memorial State Park. At the west end of Donner Lake continue up the road, where you'll see the covered railroad tracks off in the distance and rock climbers practicing on the walls. After crossing over the Rainbow Bridge, you'll arrive at the Sugar Bowl Academy building, where you'll take a left and drive past the small trailhead area on the left, and then turn right to park. **Driving east** on I-80, take the Van Norden exit and veer right onto Donner Pass Road. Drive 3.5 miles to the Mt. Judah Parking sign, which is past the Sugar Bowl's Gondola and parking area. Turn right, drive 0.2 miles, turn left at the next road to park by Lake Mary. Mountain bikes aren't allowed on the Pacific Crest Trail (PCT).

The trail begins by PCT sign with a short stroll through lush wildflowers in a woodland "fairy garden" that is magical as the early morning light filters through the trees to grace the ferns and flowers. Upon leaving the garden, the 7' tall Alpine Knotweed (*Aconogonon phytolacceafolium*) will greet you with tiny, white flowers. Then soon the trail

Thimbleberry flowers

Alpine Knotweed

Western Snake Root

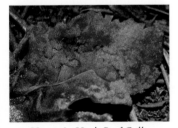

Mountain Maple Leaf Galls

makes a hairpin turn on rock-strewn switchbacks and reaches the 12–18" tall shrubs of **Western Snakeroot**. Its pink, fuzzy flowers don't seem very interesting, until viewed through a hand lens, and then Wow! . . . you'll see their "jubilant" pistils enthusiastically reaching upward towards the heavens. The pink disk flowers are held in dark phyllaries with white pappus, and their leaves are triangular-shaped. Pink Alumroot (*Heuchera rubescens*) grows out of the soil among the rocks with rounded leaves and tall stems of tiny, pink flowers with reddish sepals. Native Americans dried their astringent roots and ground them into a powder to stop bleeding wounds. The roots were also boiled for a tea to reduce fevers, nausea, and soothe a sore throat.

The Mountain Maple (*Acer glabrum*) grows by the trail, nourished by seeping water. This dioecious shrub grows up to 15' tall with inconspicuous flowers that appear in June as tiny clusters of pale green pistils without petals. On the surface of its three-lobed, toothed leaves, in July or August, you'll see red, shiny bumps that glisten in the sunlight. Check them out, because something amazing is happening! The bumps are galls created by 0.3-mm Eriophyid mites, which the mites form to protect themselves from predators as they feed on the leaves. Their feeding stimulates the plants to form the red bumps, which then hide the mites. When the leaf tissue has finished growing and becomes too tough to eat, the mites begin laying eggs and soon die.

Another cycle begins when the eggs hatch into four-legged nymphs that continue feeding for a few weeks, until they turn into adults. The young adults leave the galls from an opening under the leaves, to find other fresh leaves that are still developing. Once there are no new leaves, the mites move into tiny crevices to spend the winter in trunks, branches, and leaf buds. Come spring, they emerge with the warmth of spring to begin nibbling on the leaves again. While all this is happening, the Maple is busy forming seeds in fruits shaped like flat "wings" that change from green to reddish in the fall and then to white in the winter. In fall, their leaves turn a gorgeous red to orangish color and brighten the hillsides.

Mountain Maple fruit

The shrubby Creek Dogwood (*Cornus sericoleuca*) grows by the maples and blooms with clusters of small, white flowers on stems that

Double-flowered Honeysuckle

were used as a framework for Indian cradleboards. Double Honeysuckle (*Lonicera conjugialis*) is a shrub up to about 4′ tall and is near the dogwoods. Its small, dark red flowers are on top of fused pairs of green ovaries. "Conjugialis" is from Latin for "marriage," in reference to the fused pairs. As the ovaries mature, their red fruits swell with odd-looking "eyes" that look outward from where the styles have fallen off.

Honeysuckle fruit

Distant Views

As you approach the next horseshoe bend in the trail, look for the **Rosy Sedum** with maroon to red flowers and succulent leaves. Indigenous people ate the leaves and new shoots in early spring. Soon the trail opens with views down to Lake Mary and Lake Van Norden, which was a creek fed meadow when the emigrants arrived in the 1850s on their way to the Sacramento Valley. Magnificent

Rosy Sedum

Wind blown Jeffrey Pines

Jeffrey Pines (*Pinus jeffreyi*) grow on the hillsides pruned into beautiful shapes from the fierce winds that blow across the summit in winter. Their seeds are borne on 5–12″ long cones and feed animals and birds.

Dense shrubs of Huckleberry Oak (*Quercus vaccinifolia*) grow up to 4′ tall along the trail with small acorns tucked down in the leaves. Sticky Currant (*Ribes viscosissimum*) grows 2–4′ tall with tubular flowers that peek out from the sepals. Its glandular hairy leaves are sticky and fragrant, and its bluish black fruit is waxy coated. The *Ribes* genus is composed of gooseberries and currants, which are separated into two groups: gooseberries with prickles on their fruits and stems, and currants that lack prickles.

Mountain Pennyroyal

After the Switchbacks

In 0.9 mile from the trailhead after a series of switchbacks, the trail finally levels out and reaches a junction with the north part of the Mt. Judah Loop Trail. In July, the hillsides there are usually covered with a breathtaking expanse of gilias, lupines, mallows, and other wildflowers. The most abundant flower is usually the 18″ tall **Mountain Pennyroyal** or Coyote

Mint with white to lavender flowers that sit in leafy bracts. Their lower flower petals form a lip that extends outward to support pollinating insects. On a warm day, its leaves give off a strong mint fragrance, and the leaves can be steeped for a tasty tea. At this junction, turn left on the loop trail toward Donner Peak, which is reached on the east side of the loop. You'll return from Mt. Judah as you head north on the loop's west side.

Wavy-leaved Aster

Soon, the trail heads into the trees, where you'll see the narrow tubed, blue flowers of Slender Penstemon (*Penstemon gracilentus*), which is also called Graceful Penstemon. Nearby look for the Wavy-leaved Aster (*Eurybia integrifolia*) with purple flowers and clasping leaves. Its few ray flowers are scraggily and spaced apart, and its leaves are wavy-edged. Shortly beyond on the left is a side-trail; take it up to the rock slabs for great views of Castle Peak. Then return to the trail, and soon you'll arrive at a dirt road.

Seep garden

Head left along the road until it narrows and reaches a flowery seep garden of paintbrush, lupines, butterweeds and other flowers. Above the trail in small, mossy gardens pink Alpine Shooting Stars and yellow Primrose Monkeyflowers bloom in July. If the hillside above the trail looks reddish, climb up to see the Bud Saxifrage (*Micranthes bryoflora*). Its tiny, white flowers bloom with red sepals on the ends of downward hanging stems. The flower isn't noticeable, until seen through a hand lens. Flashy beauty attracts our attention, and tender, quiet beauty may go unnoticed until we take the time to look deeper.

Bud Saxifrage plant

Embracing Jeffrey

When you arrive at Donner Peak's flanks, walk up the rocks to the large notch at the summit for a fine view down to Donner Lake. After enjoying the view and starting

Lisa Berry

Bud Saxifrage flower

Notch on Donner Peak

down, be sure to look into the ravine below the south edge of the mountain to see where early emigrants came up with their wagons in the late 1800s on their way to Sacramento. As you are heading down, also stop at the solitary, large Jeffrey Pine growing out of the rocks and grasp one of its cones with your palm. Jeffrey's prickles bend downward, so they don't feel sharp. Ponderosa Pine prickles bend outward and are sharp, so these pines have been nicknamed "Gentle Jeffrey" and "Prickly Ponderosa." On a warm day, the sap in the Jeffrey's thickly furrowed bark gives off a rich fragrance of vanilla or butterscotch. While you're here, put your arms around its large trunk to give it a hug and rest your head against its massive trunk to inhale its delicious fragrance. Give Jeffrey your thanks and then close your eyes and become very still, until you feel its powerful energy flowing into you and yours into it.

More Switchbacks up Mt. Judah

After returning to the trail, either head back for the shorter hike option or head left to continue on to Mt. Judah. In July, you'll find gorgeous,

Rock Fringe

bright pink **Rock Fringe** cascading down the hillsides. Check out the flowers, and you'll see that on some, the styles are bent out of the way to prevent self-pollination. After its pollen has been released, the style moves to the center, and its dark pink stigma opens into four lobes to receive pollen.

As you climb up the switchbacks along flower covered hillsides and lichen-colored volcanic formations, you'll see many Azure Penstemons, some of which are pink. These may be hybrids of blue Azure

Penstemon and pink Mountain Pride. I haven't found an Azure Penstemon with this color anywhere else at Tahoe. You'll also find the common Brewer's Golden Aster (*Eucephalus breweri*) with yellow disk flowers on scraggily plants. After the switchbacks, the trail straightens out and gradually heads straight up to the mountaintop, through more Mule's Ears in June and July and past blue Explorer's Gentians in August. At the top, you'll see Donner Lake and distant mountains. In June and July, you'll find many alpine plants in bloom on the

Azure Penstemons

barren mountaintop as you are treated to the brisk, exhilarating air. You'll see yellow Sulphur Flowers (*Erigeron umbellatum*) hunkered down to avoid the intense winds. After pollination, their flowers turn deep red to absorb heat to nurture their maturing seeds. Globe Gilia (*Ipomopsis congesta*) with tiny white flowers, blue anthers, and small fan-shaped leaves, grows near bright yellow Woolly Sunflowers (*Eriophyllum lanatum*) and tiny, white flowers in red bracts of the Alpine Paintbrush (*Castilleja nana*). **Potbelly Owl's Clover** is 4–10″ tall with clusters of green and pink bracts that surround tiny, two-lipped flowers. The upper lip is pink and pointed and encloses the reproductive parts, and the lower lip is white and rounded like a tiny belly. It's a hemiparasite that carries out photosynthesis, but also has specialized roots that penetrate the roots of nearby plants for their nutrients and water.

Globe Gilia

Potbelly Owl's Clover

Flowers line the trail

Heading Down from the Summit

After the summit, a gradual descent on switchbacks heads down the south side of Mt. Judah where you'll find the California Sunflower (*Helianthella californica*), which is easily identified by its two leafy bracts just below the flowers and its long, numerous, dark green leaves. After the switchbacks end, the trail levels out, and you'll arrive at the junction with the west side of the Mt. Judah Loop. You can turn right to head north back to your car or turn left to take a short walk to Roller Pass. This is where the first emigrants in 1846 pulled their wagons 1,600′ up from Coldstream Valley using oxen and rollers. The view from the pass down into the valley and south along the PCT to Tinker Knob is spectacular. When I'm here, I gaze down into the valley and remember with gratitude how Walter Hewlett and his wife,

California Sunflower

View along the Pacific Crest Trail in May

Esther, stepped in and purchased the land to preserve it forever after a plan had been proposed earlier for development with condominiums and a ski resort.

After visiting the pass, head back on the trail and continue north along the west side of the loop past wet gardens of flowers that grow in colorful, luxurious drifts down the hillsides. Under the alders at stream crossings, you'll find the 4–12″ tall **Brewer's Bishop's Cap** with round, basal leaves and strange, ½″ wide, pale green to yellowish flowers with delicate, pinnately lobed petals. A greenish white, lobed stigma rises out of the flower's center, and its anthers are white nubbins that rest on the sepals below the petals. It's named for the fruit capsule, which resembles a Catholic Bishop's hat. As you pass through Red Fir forests with lime green lichen on their trunks, look for the bright red Snow Plant, reddish Coral Root Orchid, and 6″ tall Little Prince's Pine (*Chimaphila menziesii*) with nodding, white flowers that turn pink as they age. It is also called "Pipsissewa" after its Cree name "pipisiskweu," for "it breaks it into pieces." The Cree people used it to break up gallstones. Its evergreen leaves are toothed at the tip and were used by Native

Brewer's Bishop's Cap

Little Prince's Pine

Mt. Judah Trail in fall

Americans as an astringent, antibiotic, and diuretic to treat inflammation of the urinary track.

After the forest, more flowery hillsides and dry chaparral-covered slopes appear. When the trail arrives at the junction you took earlier toward Donner Peak, pick up the trail that you came in on by heading straight down the hill to return to your car. The Mt. Judah Loop is one of Tahoe's most beautiful trails, and though June through August are the best months for wildflowers, fall is also gratifying when the days are brisk and windy, and the ferns, deciduous trees, and shrubs turn orange and yellow. At this time, red California Fuchsias offer nectar to south migrating hummingbirds, and deep blue Explorer's Gentians grace the slopes, both saying goodbye to the flower season with a final, exuberant blast of color.

#6 Castle Valley to Round Valley

Castle Peak

One Way: Approx. 2.5 miles
Map: NG: Tahoe National Forest, Sierra Buttes/Donner Pass
Trail Begins/Ends: 7,200'/7,880'
Wildflower Season: late June through August

Castle Valley lies below Castle Peak, which is named for the volcanic extrusions on its jagged summit that resemble the turrets of a medieval castle. Castle Peak's west-side trail leads to two lush valleys with meandering creeks that flow through splendid wildflower meadows. Castle Valley is reached first on a short hike and is a quiet, accessible place to picnic and spend hours with canvas and paints or to photograph the lush flowers. This valley is especially beautiful, because its meadow is backdropped by the sheer, dramatic cliffs of Castle Peak. Round Valley's larger, flowery meadow is reached after Castle Valley and looks up to the long, open ridgeline between the Castle and Basin Peaks.

93

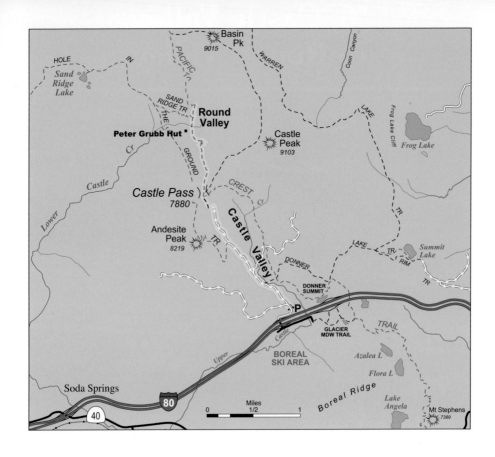

Featured Flowers

Graceful Cinquefoil (*Potentilla gracilis*)
Bigleaf Avens (*Geum macrophyllum*)
Lewis' Monkeyflower (*Mimulus lewisii*)
Wandering Daisy (*Erigeron glacialis*)
Lemmon's Paintbrush (*Castilleja lemmonii*)
Corn Lily (*Veratrum californicum*)

Trailhead Directions: **From Truckee heading west** on Interstate 80, take the Boreal Ridge exit after the rest area. At the off-ramp stop sign, turn right and drive uphill to the parking area. **Heading east** on I-80, take the Castle Peak/Boreal Ridge exit. Turn left at the off-ramp and head under the freeway to the road up to the parking.

The trail begins by the trailhead sign and a gate that is opened after the snow melts. It follows an old road below Andesite Ridge through conifers and past lavender Wandering Daisies, pink Pussy Paws, Sierran Stickseeds, and tiny pink Whisker Brush. In 0.3 mile, the trail arrives at Castle Valley's meadow and dirt turnout. Along the meadow's creek in June and July, will be nodding Crimson Columbines, Large-leaf Lupines, Elephant's Heads, Arrowleaf Butterweeds, and the 5' tall plants of Mountain Larkspur (*Delphinium glaucum*). Its dark blue flowers grow along glaucous (waxy coated) stems. "Delphinium" is from Latin for "dolphin," and if you look at the flowers in bud, with some imagination, you'll see tiny dolphins "floating" on top of their stems.

Graceful Cinquefoil blooms in wet, grassy areas with bright yellow flowers and 5 uniform petals. It grows up to 2' tall with fan-shaped, palmate leaves that are divided into five to seven serrated leaflets. Sierran Woodbeauty (*Drymocallis glandulosa*) is similar, though its leaves are pinnate. Its flowers are pale yellow in North Tahoe, but bloom pale yellow or white in South Tahoe. **Bigleaf Avens** grows nearby up to 3' tall with similar, bright yellow flowers that form unusual, green, ball-shaped fruits covered with showy styles. "Macrophyllum" refers to the large, terminal leaflet by the smaller, various sized, pinnate leaflets, which is a way to identify this plant.

"Dolphins floating"

Graceful Cinquefoil

Bigleaf Avens fruit

Bigleaf Avens

Sierran Woodbeauty

An Animate Stigma

After returning to the road, you'll pass seep gardens with Tahoe's tallest monkeyflower, which grows up to 4′ tall. **Lewis' Monkeyflower** has tubular blossoms with 5 flaring petal lobes. Hairy, yellow ridges line the lower petal to entice pollinators. "Lewis" honors Captain Meriwether Lewis, who collected it in 1805 on the famous Lewis and Clark Expedition. "Mimulus" is from Latin "mimus," for "comic actor" or "mime." "Monkey" is for its supposed resemblance to a little monkey, happily smiling out at life.

Lewis Monkeyflower

Lewis Monkeyflower stigma

Take a moment to find a comfortable spot to sit down and look closely at several of its flowers. A tiny white stigma without an obvious style sits just above the throat's opening and is pressed against the upper petals. Its stigma is composed of 2 tiny, attached lobes, but when the lobes close, they look like a single lobe. It's fun to look at the stigma, because this is a discerning plant. When an insect touches its stigma with pollen from another Lewis Monkeyflower, the stigma lobes close against the upper petals and remain closed to secure the pollen for fertilization. But if the lobes have been touched with the wrong pollen, i.e. pollen from some other flower species, the lobes will re-open within a few minutes to wait for the right pollen. This closure is fun, because the opened stigma can be touched by a child with a blade of grass to watch it close and then wait to watch it re-open.

Arrowleaf Butterweed

This temporary closure reduces the chance of self-pollination, after an insect has picked up the flower's own pollen during the time it's rummaging about in the flower searching for nectar.

Hillsides of Color and Song

If you hike here after a year of good snowfall, the wet gardens along the road will be blooming with Corn Lilies and bright yellow Arrowleaf Butterweed (*Senecio triangularis*). Butterweeds grow up to about 4′ tall with leaves that are arrowhead-shaped. You'll also find the 3–4′ tall shrubs of fragrant, pink flowered Mountain Spiraea (*Spiraea splendens*). Be sure to inhale its perfume, which might make you want to compare the fragrance of all the various flowers and leaves along the trail. The beautiful fragrance of flowers floats on the air like music, which is no less beautiful, because our ears don't pick up their "fragrant songs." Checking out the various scents of

Mountain Spiraea

flowers and leaves, can lead us into a deeper connection with plants, while toughening up our knees a bit, which is a must for botanists and wildflower photographers.

Scientists are now discovering what our indigenous ancestors have known for thousands of years . . . that plants communicate with each other and each plant has its own song. This may seem unbelievable, until we realize that plants send out acoustical signals from ocillations within their cells as one way of communicating with other plants. Researchers have developed machines that can interpret these signals as songs, which are within our range of hearing. See p. 266. This opens up a whole new way of relating to plants and an exciting, deeper way to experience plants. I've heard their songs through these machines. I needed to "prove" this for myself, so I asked to listen to different plants to see if their songs would differ. Indeed they did, and each song I listened too was exquisite with its own ethereal beauty. Perhaps the songs of plants aren't too surprising, for as Steven Buhner writes, "All forms of life are intelligent as self-organized, embedded systems, all communicating with one another." . . . And many of them ". . . predate the emergence of the human species by hundreds of millions of years. They must have been doing something all that time, you know, besides waiting for us to appear."

Continuing on to Castle Pass

In 1.5 miles from the trailhead, the road reaches a dirt parking area and the unsigned trail for a short, steep climb up to 7,880′ Castle Pass. From there, you'll head north straight downhill toward Round Valley. (The trail to the right leads to the Castle and Basin Peaks.) As the trail descends, look for patches of bright pink Mountain Pride

Mountain Pride

Wandering Daisy

(*Penstemon newberryi*), which begins blooming in late June. When you arrive at the huge, magnificent Western White Pine (*Pinus monticola*), be sure to give it a hug. At this point the trail continues through Red Firs and Lodgepole Pines alongside white Yampahs, Azure Penstemons, and Scarlet Gilias. You'll also find beautiful displays of the 6–18″ tall **Wandering Daisy** . Its 1″ wide flowers bloom with lavender petals (ray flowers) and golden disk flowers. Its simple leaves are generally basal. If you turn the flower over, you'll see glands on their reflexed phyllaries. If you give this daisy your loving attention, it may just smile right back at you with delight!

A "smiling" daisy

Arriving at Round Meadow

Soon after entering the meadow, the trail passes the Peter Grubb Hut on the left in the trees. The hut was built in 1938–1939 by friends and family in memory of Peter Grubb, who was an avid skier and mountaineer from San Francisco. There are three such Sierra Club huts at Tahoe, available to its members or in emergencies (info@clairtappaanlodge.com).

Peter Grubb Hut

I once spent New Year's eve in the hut with friends after we skied into the valley during the day. As night-time came and the moon rose, we put on our skis and went out to connect with the night's stark beauty. Under a star-lit sky, we made our way through snow that sparkled with millions of tiny "rainbows" or actually "moonbows" on the hoar frost. This type of frost creates elongated ice crystals that form when there is moisture in the air during subfreezing nights. They resemble vertical pieces of glass shards, and as we skied through the snow, we tapped the icy bits of frosty "glass" with our ski poles. They shattered like broken glass, tinkling as they collapsed onto the snow. It was a magical way to say goodby to the old year and greet the new one.

Lower Castle Creek flows through Round Valley to nurture the meadow's large flower community. In some years, **Lemmon's Paintbrush** covers the meadow with swaths of vivid, pink-tipped bracts that enclose its pale yellow to greenish yellow flowers. Its lance-like, hairy leaves grow vertically along a 12″ stem. The tubular, yellowish green flowers have two fused upper petals and lower swollen-shaped petals. The stamens bend forward with pinkish anthers to offer their gift of pollen grains. Once the anthers have released the pollen, the style elongates and appears at the tip of the flower to further entice pollinators.

Lemmon's
Paintbrush

fused
upper
petals

Lisa Berry

This Paintbrush is named after John Lemmon (1832–1908), a botanist who studied and collected plants in the western states with his wife, Sarah Plummer Lemmon (1836–1923). Sarah was also a botanist and nationally recognized for her botanical illustrations. With her husband and a guide, they once scaled the unnamed, tallest peak in the Santa Catalina Mountains near Tucson, Arizona. After Sarah discovered a new flower on the mountain, local Native Americans named it Mount Lemmon to honor her. Sarah worked to gain statewide recognition for the California Poppy and wrote the bill that passed the legislature in 1903, naming it the California State Flower. The Lemmons created an herbarium in their home, which they later donated to the University of California in Berkeley, which became the Jepson Herbarium.

One of the showiest flowers in the meadow is the white flowered, toxic **Corn Lily** that grows up to 5′ tall. It covers huge areas with large clusters of flowers, but it requires deep snow or good rains to blossom abundantly. Its flowers bloom with 6 identical petals and sepals, marked with dark green nectar glands. White stamens flare outward, topped with yellow anthers, which turn brown after releasing their pollen.

Corn Lilies

Corn Lily flowers
and buds

White-flowered Bog Orchid

Another white flower in the meadow is the fragrant White-flowered Bog Orchid (*Platanthera dilatata*), which grows along the creek, with tiny, white flowers clustered along 1' to 2' tall stems. A long, thin spur extends backward from the lower petal. The spur contains nectar to attract moths, who can reach into the spur with a proboscis to sip the nectar. Most people think of orchids as exotic flowers found mainly in the tropics. Though most orchids are tropical, others live in various environments worldwide with at least six species in Tahoe.

Orchids belong to one of the largest flower families with close to 35,000 species. They vary in size from 30" to tiny flowers only a few millimeters in size. They have developed unusual shapes, because of a closely evolving relationship with specific pollinators. Some orchids depend upon only one insect species for pollination, which creates beautiful and unusual adaptive responses in both the flower and insect. The fragrant Angraecum Orchid in Madagascar has a 12" long nectar spur, and when Darwin first saw it, he theorized that there must be an insect pollinator with a 12" long proboscis. It seems logical, but botanists laughed at him, until the pollinator was found 50 years later. It is the Long Tongued Hawk Moth with a

Flowers in Round Valley

proboscis over 12" long. Imagine its young moth uncoiling its long "tongue" and getting confused about how to put it back! Other orchids have formed flowers that look and smell like a female fly that tricks the male fly into "mating" with the flower, and in doing so he pollinates it.

As you wander in the meadow exploring the different habitats and their flowers be sure to stop to enjoy the detail of each flower. If you're with a child, ask him or her to inhale its fragrance and to feel its leaves. Ask what it might be like to be a flower in this meadow, to have feet in the mud and a face buzzed by bees! Also suggest that they give each flower a name and look at it through a hand lens. You might also just enjoy watching the clouds float over head as you lie together nestled in the meadow's beauty. Learning the adult names of plants can come later, after they've chosen their own special names for their plants. As John Burroughs once said, "Knowledge without love will not stick. But if love comes first, knowledge is sure to follow."

Ridgeline between Basin and Castle Peaks

Loop: Approximately 6 miles
Trail Begins/High Point: 7,200'/9,103'
Map: NG: Tahoe National Forest, Sierra Buttes/Donner Pass
Wildflower Season: June to September

Sitting by the orange and yellow, lichen-colored pinnacles near Castle Peak, one could begin the day watching the sun rise in pink splendor over shadowed eastern ridges or end the day watching it sink far into the west in the late afternoon alpenglow. This fabulous trail follows two ridgelines to ascend two peaks, each with their own dramatic vistas and colorful gardens of alpine cushion plants, lush meadow flowers, and slopes of bright pink Sierra Primroses. Basin Peak's summit is reached on a short uphill hike through waist high flowers that bloom in July, after which, the trail heads down through a Hemlock forest to reach the large, beautiful meadow in Round Valley.

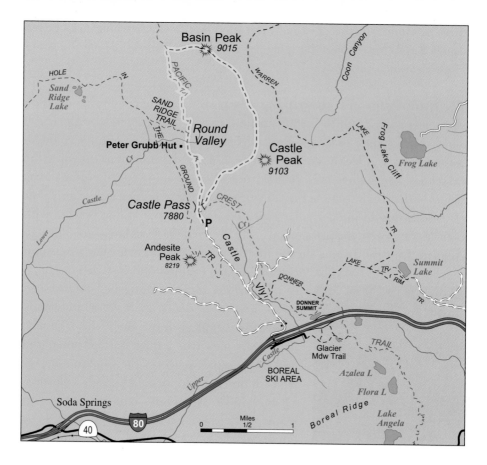

Featured Flowers

Drummond's Anemone (*Anemone drummondii*)

Pink Star Onion (*Allium platycaule*)

Narrow-tube Skyrocket (*Ipomopsis tenuituba*)

Leichtlin's Mariposa Lily (*Calochortus leichtlinii*)

Whitney's Locoweed (*Astragalus whitneyi*)

Silky Raillardella (*Raillardella argentea*)

Trailhead Directions: **From Truckee** heading west on Interstate 80, take the Boreal Ridge exit. At the off-ramp stop sign, turn right onto an unmarked, blacktopped road and head uphill to the Forest Service gate. **Heading east** on Interstate 80, take the Boreal Ridge/Castle Peak exit. Turn left at the off-ramp and drive under the freeway, past the I-80 westbound off-ramp and up the blacktopped road to the gate. The gate is locked during the winter, but opens after the snow melts. Call the Truckee Ranger District of the Tahoe National Forest to confirm the gate is open. From the gate, drive 1.5 miles up the old road until it ends in a dirt parking area below Castle Pass. (You'll pass the Hole in the Ground Trail sign along the way.) High-clearance cars only.

The trail begins near the parking area on the unsigned trail that makes a short, steep climb up to 7,880' Castle Pass. At the pass, head right (east) along the ridgeline to Castle Peak. From there, the trail continues along a second, longer ridgeline to Basin Peak. One of the best times to enjoy the ridgelines' alpine flowers is June or soon after the snow melts. Alpine plants bloom earlier than those in the valley, because snow is gone earlier at higher elevations due to intense solar rays and fierce winds. Valley flowers with their less exposed, deeper snow usually bloom later from late June through August. The trail begins on the first ridgeline with spectacular vistas and colorful, alpine cushion plants. One charming, 6" tall cushion plant is Butterballs (*Eriogonum ovalifolium*) with dense mats of white-woolly leaves. As is typical in the Buckwheat Family, its flowers lack true petals. Instead, their red and white sepals perform the function of petals with flowers that form ball-shaped clusters. **Drummond's Anemone** blooms nearby on plants 4–12" tall. Its inch-wide flowers have white, petal-like sepals that are usually blue beneath. It's in the Buttercup Family; many members of this family also lack true petals. Its yellow pistils and stamens cluster in the flower's center, optimistically awaiting visits by the few insects that dare to venture out so early in the season. Later, you'll find its round, hairy fruits covered with little nubbins and dried-up protruding styles.

Butterballs

Finding the **Pink Star Onion** is another treat that makes my heart happy. Its flowers resemble pink stars in dense, ball-shaped clusters. Their curling, strap-like leaves often form a "loving heart" as they embrace the pink blossoms. Gently squeeze the edible leaves to inhale their strong onion smell. Also look for the low

Drummond's Anemone   Anemone fruit

growing Alpine Dusty Maiden (Chaenatis douglasii var. alpina) with woolly, pinnate leaves and pink and white disk flowers only. It also prefers dry, rocky habitats and often grows in tight clumps.

Pink Star Onion

Algae and Fungi in Cooperation

Soon, you'll arrive at rugged volcanic extrusions in a variety of shapes, from an old man patiently awaiting eternity to a resting dog peacefully surveying the landscape. Splotches of orange, yellow, and black lichen decorate the rocks, and although the splotches may seem lifeless, they are actually two primitive plants, fungi and algae, that live in a symbiotic union. View them with your hand lens, and you'll enter a whole new world. The algae and fungi live together, with the fungi putting out thread-like rhizoids, called "hyphae." The hyphae grip the rocks and produce strong acids that decompose the rocks and release their minerals. With the minerals, air moisture, and sunshine, the algae carries out photosynthesis to sustain them both, with the fungi "providing the home," and the algae "putting dinner on the table." By decomposing the rocks, fungi help to create precious soil, which gathers in small cracks where tiny plants can begin their lives. When these plants die, they decompose to create additional soil. With time, larger plants colonize the rocks and bring varied plant life and color to the larger niches in the volcanic formations.

Alpine Dusty Maidens

Other Ridgeline Flowers

In the spring and summer of 2015, during California's fourth year of drought, I was grateful for the spring snows and summer rains that gave rise to a gorgeous display of wildflowers all along both ridgelines.

Lichen decorate the lava rocks

Mule's Ears and Lupines

Woolly Sunflowers

Narrow-tube Sky Rocket

Clustered Broomrape

Spreading Phlox, Sulphur Flowers, Scarlet Gilias, and Mule's Ears lit up the trail on both ridges with views down to Round Valley's green meadow. Along the ridgelines, one of the brightest flowers is the Woolly Sunflower (*Eriophyllum lanatum*). A single bright yellow flower grows on each 5–12" stem above its woolly leaves. Its ray flowers are a darker yellow at the base and three-lobed at the tip.

As the trail climbs more steeply, you'll see the **Narrow-tube Skyrocket.** "Tenuituba" is Latin for "slender trumpet," after its slender, tubular-shaped flowers with flaring petals. It grows 12–24" tall with pinnate leaves. In this area, look also for the small, leafless plants of the Clustered Broomrape (*Orobanche facsiculata*) on the trail's right side. It's a charming, little plant, unless you happen to be the Sagebrush that it parasitizes! Its yellow, tubular flowers sit on 1–2" tall stems. Its seeds fall onto the soil and remain dormant for many years, until they are exposed to a chemical, deposited in the soil by a nearby Sagebrush or other preferred host plant. This chemical causes the seeds to germinate and send out roots that eventually find and penetrate the roots of Sagebrush or other nearby hosts to absorb water and nutrients. Soil fungi act as intermediaries to make this connection between the broomrapes and their preferred host plants.

Ascending Castle Peak or Taking the Trail Fork
Soon the trail becomes steeper but continue on, because the ridgeline leading to Basin Peak isn't far, and its flowers will "blow your mind" in a year of abundant snow or rain. Castle Peak's 9,103' summit has gorgeous vistas and so do the ridgelines.

The last rocky, exposed segment of the ascent to the summit can be scary for those not used to the exposure of steep drop-offs, but there is another trail, mentioned below, for those who want to avoid going to the summit. After reaching Castle Peak's summit and enjoying the scenery, there is another short trail down the north side of the mountain to reach the ridgeline trail to Basin Peak.

Heartleaf Arnica

The alternate trail is reached at a trail fork about 1 mile from the trailhead. The right fork leads to the summit and the left enters the forest to gradually follow the contours of the mountain up to the ridgeline for Basin Peak. Along the way, you'll find very special flowers. Among them will be the Heartleaf Arnica (*Arnica cordifolia*). It grows up to 12″ tall with bright yellow ray flowers that surround golden disk flowers, and its fragrant, hairy, heart-shaped leaves grow in 2–4 opposite pairs along the stem. You'll also see the Sierra Primrose (*Primula suffrutescens*) with bright pink flowers that sparkle with a yellow, bulls-eye center. It grows 4–6″ tall with basal, evergreen leaves that are protected from the winter's freezing temperatures by deep snow. Soon you'll reach an open hillside, which blooms with dazzling cushion plants. As the trail reaches

Sierra Primrose

the ridgeline, it merges with the trail off Castle Peak and continues north along the generally level and spectacular ridgeline to Basin Peak.

Waking the Ridgeline

Cushion plants grow along the ridgeline nearby the taller plants of Mule's Ears, Blue Flax, Hot-rock Penstemon, and King's Sandwort (*Eremogone kingii*). A cushion plant's form protects it from being torn apart by heavy winds, and its compact growth retains the day's warmth at night. The taller plants adapt

Ridgeline cushion plants

Mariposa Lilies

Whitney's Locoweed

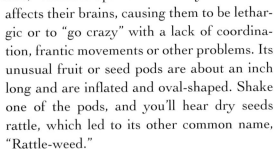

Alpine Paintbrush

to the high elevation winds by bending instead of resisting. One of life's lessons!

One of the sweetest plants on the ridgeline is **Leichtlin's Mariposa Lily**. At this high elevation, it only grows about 2″ tall. Its white petals are marked with a dark spot above each golden nectar gland. Other species of calochortus lilies, which don't grow here, vary in color from our white one to yellow, red or pink. "Calochortus" is from the Greek "kallos" for "beautiful" and "chortus" for "grass," referring to its grass-like leaves and beautiful flowers. Its seeds and bulbs were staple foods roasted and eaten by all the California Indians.

Along the ridgeline, volcanic rocks form goulish shapes and there are distant mountain vistas and lovely, expansive views into the green meadows below on both sides of the ridgeline. Along the trail, you'll probably be surprised when you come upon the fruit of **Whitney's Locoweed**. This prostrate plant lounges on the sandy soil with soft, hairy, pinnate leaves, purple to white flowers, and inflated fruits. "Locoweed" refers to a toxic substance in the plants of this genus that causes animals who eat them to go "loco," which is Spanish for "crazy." The toxin affects their brains, causing them to be lethargic or to "go crazy" with a lack of coordination, frantic movements or other problems. Its unusual fruit or seed pods are about an inch long and are inflated and oval-shaped. Shake one of the pods, and you'll hear dry seeds rattle, which led to its other common name, "Rattle-weed."

You'll also find the Alpine Paintbrush (*Castilleja nana*), which grows 4–6″ tall with tightly clustered, white flowers, enclosed in red, purplish, white or yellow bracts. The **Silky Raillardella** is a shiny leaved plant with yellow disk flowers that give rise to extended styles with lobed, curled stigmas. It grows up to 6" tall with silver, silky leaves that are basal and up to 3" long. Along the ridgeline, among these flowers, you'll see the twisted trunk of an old Whitebark Pine (*Pinus albicaulis*) barely holding onto life. Its few, living branches and green needles grip its twisted branches. I've watched it age over the years and have felt sad for its struggle, but its determination to survive is inspiring. Near the pine, you'll find the small, tubular, bluish purple flowers of the Whorled Penstemon (*Penstemon heterodoxus*). Its glandular-hairy flowers whorl around 6–12" tall stems, and its white throat attracts insects to the flower's center.

Silky Raillardella

Reaching Basin Peak

As you approach 9015′ Basin Peak, you'll see Brewer's Lupines, Hot-rock Penstemons, and more Woolly Sunflowers. Looking back toward Castle Peak can be spectacular with Mule's Ears, Spurred Lupines, and Pink Skyrockets. Before the trail heads up Basin Peak's flank, walk northeast through the conifers to the rocky slopes beyond the trees to see large groups of Sierra Primroses flowing down the rock-strewn mountain's east side. Look also for the whitish flowers of the Long-petaled Lewisia (*Lewisia longipetala*) growing among the rocks. A white, lobed stigma rises out of the flower's center, and its anthers are red to golden. Red glands top the green sepals, and its leaves are long, narrow, and succulent.

Whorled Penstemon

Long-petaled Lewisia

Sierra Primroses

*Roundleaf
Snowberry
shrubs*

*Snowberry's
bell-shaped
flowers*

Mountain Hemlock

Round Valley's Corn Lilies

After returning to the trail, take the short climb up to Basin Peak past the 4' tall shrubs of Roundleaf Snowberry (*Symphoricarpos rotundifolius*), with small, bell-shaped flowers. It's named for its white fruit, which contains saponin that is mildly toxic to humans, though Quail, Robins, Grouse, and other birds consume it. The short, rocky "mountain goat" trail to the Peak's 9,015' summit offers more gorgeous vistas. From there, the trail leads down the northwest flank and then south to meet up with the Pacific Crest Trail (PCT) and the west side of Round Valley's large meadow. This gradual trail has its own pristine, windswept beauty as it winds its way past rounded, open hillsides of clumping, native grasses and wildflowers and past grand old groves of Mountain Hemlock (*Tsuga mertensiana*). This is one of our most graceful conifers. Its tip droops as if to declare it has expended all its energy on the magnificent growth below. Like a true alpine mountaineer, this tree prefers rugged exposures on windy ridges. Its cones mature within one year instead of the normal two years for most conifers. They shed their seeds in the fall, and the cones fall to the ground to disintegrate and recycle their nutrients in the soil.

Completing the Trail's Loop

After passing through the forests, you'll be on the PCT by Round Valley meadow and will arrive at a junction with the Sand Ridge Trail that heads west. Continue straight for a leiurely meander through the meadow. In June or July, Corn Lilies (*Veratrum californicum*) put on a startling display, with hundreds of 5–6' tall plants blooming with large clusters of white flowers. Along the creeks you'll find shooting stars, arnicas, paintbrushes, and lupines blooming in a riot of color as described on the Castle Valley to Round Valley hike. As the PCT continues south along the meadow, it passes the Sierra Club's Peter Grubb Hut. After the trail leaves the valley, it climbs up along a series of switchbacks

Looking back at Castle Peak from the area by Basin Peak

on the easily followed trail back to Castle Pass to complete the loop and return to your car. You'll probably be tired when you arrive at your car, but exhilarated by a day spent in such beauty.

King's Sandwort grows on Basin Peak with needle-like leaves

#8 Sagehen Creek

Quamash Camas Lilies in Sagehen Meadow

One Way: 2.5 miles
Trail Begins/Ends: 6,100'/6,000'
Map: AM: Lake Tahoe Basin
Wildflower Season: May to August

Sagehen Creek has a peacefulness and beauty that isn't diminished even with other people on this popular trail. If winter snows have been generous, a breath-taking expanse of Camas Lilies bloom at the trail's end in a big meadow by the creek. A small, boggy meadow with unusual flowers can be visited, before the main trail. Large golden Balsamroots cover hillsides down to the creek-sides. Summer brings warm days with Bluebirds catching insects on the wing and Beaver kits swimming through the waters by their lodge. In fall as the weather cools, Sagehen becomes a quiet, peaceful place to enjoy fall color, before winter snows turn it all into a blanket of white.

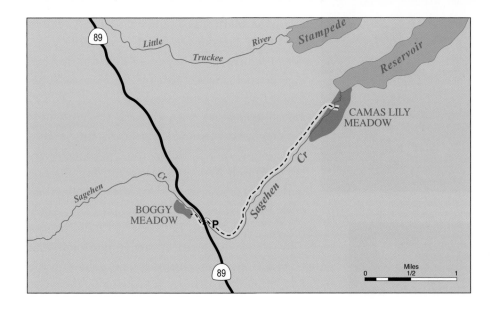

Featured Flowers
Western Polemonium (*Polemonium occidentale*)
Marsh Marigold (*Caltha leptosepala*)
Alpine Gentian (*Gentiana newberryi*)
Brown's Peony (*Paeonia brownii*)
Star Lavender (*Hydrophylllum alpestre*)
Quamash Camas Lily (*Camassia quamash*)

Trailhead Directions: **From Truckee** on Interstate 80, take the Sierraville exit north onto Highway 89. At the first roundabout, follow the sign toward Donner Pass Road. At the next two roundabouts, head toward Sierraville. The unsigned Sagehen trailhead is reached in 7.4 miles from I-80, just after the highway crosses a cement bridge over Sagehen Creek. Turn down into the parking area on the east side of the highway. This user-created trail is not found on maps but is easy to follow along the north side of Sagehen Creek. The Sagehen Field Station, upstream on Sagehen Creek, offers periodic events and programs for the public, but is not open for general public visits (www.sagehen.ucnrs.org).

Visiting the Boggy Meadow
After parking, first cross back over the highway to find in May strange flowers of pink Steer's Head (*Dicentra uniflora*) carpeting the ground near the road, above its gray green leaves. Then take the short trail from there

Marsh Marigolds

Alpine Gentian

Western Polemonium

Bog Saxifrage

along the south side of upper Sagehen Creek to the boggy meadow to see its unusual flowers. Tread lightly in its boggy gardens on downed logs or rocks, when possible. In May to June, you'll find tiny, pink Elephant's Head (*Pedicularis groenlandica*) with flowers that resemble an elephant's rounded forehead, tiny trunk, and floppy ears. Nearby, the 1½" wide flowers of **Marsh Marigold** bloom in May or June without petals; instead they attract pollinators with their white, petal-like sepals. The sepals are white to our eyes, but bees and other insects with ultraviolet vision see attractive markings that entice them. One early spring morning, here in the meadow, I found the marigolds growing by the creek with their flowers gazing up at me with "curiosity" through a thin sheet of ice, which had formed over them during the night in the freezing temperatures. As the sun came up and melted the ice, the flowers seemed happy and undamaged by the ice.

Later in the season, the White-flowered Bog Orchid (*Platanthera dilatata*), which smells like vanilla, blooms on 2' tall stalks. Each flower supports a long nectar spur to attract moths, who reach down into the spur with a proboscis to sip its nectar. Another rarely seen flower is the **Alpine Gentian**, which grows 1–4" tall with a white flower that resembles a wide-mouthed vase. Its petals are speckled on the inside and decorated with tiny fringes between the petals.

In very boggy areas, you'll find the **Western Polemonium**. Its solitary stems are up to 3' tall and support graceful flowers, each with a thread-like style that extends downward. Delicate stamens reach outward to show off their yellow anthers. Also check out the 2–3' tall stalks and the sepals of the Bog Saxifrage (*Micranthes oregana*) to see their glandular hairs. These sticky glands exude a tiny drop of liquid from the tip of each hair to discourage poor pollinators from climbing up the plant to "steal" the pollen. Crawling insects lose the precious pollen as they move through grasses, and they are inefficient, because they randomly visit different flower species. Bees are good pollinators, because they don't lose the pollen as they fly from flower to flower, and many species of bees tend to focus on only one flower species during a pollinating session.

Mountain Rose

Returning to the Main Trail

After returning to the parking area, pick up the unmarked trail along the creek where in July, you'll find the fragrant flowers of the Mountain Rose (*Rosa woodsii*) on thorny shrubs 4–5' tall. Its five-petaled pink blossoms seem to float gracefully among the leaves. In the fall, its flowers have matured into orange to red rose hips that are high in Vitamin C and were brewed into a tea by the Washoes. Look in the grassy areas past the roses for Richardson's Geranium (*Geranium richardsonii*). Its white to pale lavender flowers are streaked with purple and grow up to 2' tall. Golden hairs decorate its petals by the yellow ovary. Green, needle-tipped sepals peek out from between the petals. Pink to golden anthers on red filaments extend outward, waiting to distribute their golden, life-giving pollen. Nearby, the charming little flowers of Self Heal (*Prunella vulgaris*) bloom tucked in brownish purple bracts, on 6" or taller stems. Each flower resembles a little girl with her arms bent downward above a ragged skirt.

Richardson's Geranium

Self Heal

In forested areas, Rocky Mountain Butterweed (*Packera streptanthifolia*) grows up to 12" tall with yellow flowers. With your hand lens, see if you can find tiny, white hairs in the axils of its leaves. In moist areas of the forest, Baker's Violet (*Viola bakeri*) grows with deep yellow

Rocky Mountain Butterweed

Baker's Violet

Mahala Mat

Brown's Peony

Star Lavender

flowers that may be marked with brownish maroon on the back of the upper two petals. In sunnier areas of the forest in June, you'll find the blue to purplish flowers of Mahala Mat (*Ceanothus prostratus*) with spoon-shaped petals that radiate outward from its inward-curled, petal-like sepals. Its small, prickly, holly-like leaves create dense mats that act as nurseries for seeds that fall from the trees, keeping them cool and moist until they germinate.

In early June, look for the unusual, nodding flowers of **Brown's Peony**. If you miss them in bloom, you may still find their swollen seed pods in July. **Star Lavender** grows nearby with flowers that snuggle beneath the leaves, like chicks clustered under a mother hen's wings. Stamens protrude from its flowers, giving them a fuzzy look. Indigenous people ate the leaves and young shoots raw or cooked. Western Waterleaf (*Hydrophyllum occidentale*) is closely related with similar white to lavender flowers that bloom above its sometimes spotted leaves.

If you are on the trail in June and July, you'll be treated to the large, bright yellow flowers of Mountain Mule's Ears and Balsamroots, which in full bloom paint the hillsides yellow. See p. 154. Interspersed with them will be the 18″ tall, toxic plants of Sand Corn (*Toxicoscordion paniculatum*). Their grass-like leaves are long and narrow, and their creamy yellow flowers are unusual, because some are male with stamens only, while others have both stamens and female pistils.

Down close to the ground you'll find many small flowers that could easily go unnoticed by the casual hiker. The purple to lavender blue blossoms of Low Phacelia (*Phacelia humilis*) grow on plants 2–10″ tall with hairy, lance-like leaves. Sometimes they carpet large areas on the sandy floor with hundreds of delicate flowers.

Sagehen Balsamroots

Sand Corn

The tiniest flower, Staining Collomia (*Collomia tinctoria*), is only about ⅛" inch wide with white to pink petals and blue anthers. Its narrow, extended, reddish brown tube supports spreading petals. Use your hand lens to see their delicate markings and to go deeply into "their world."

Low Phacelia

Trailside Shrubs

In dry habitats, Greenleaf Manzanita (*Arctostaphylos patula*) grows 5-6' tall with pink, urn-shaped flowers. You'll also find Mountain Sagebrush (*Artemisia tridentata*) and Bitterbrush (*Purshia tridentata*). Sagebrush is a common, fragrant-leaved plant up to 2–3' tall with tiny, creamy flowers on long, naked stems. Bitterbrush grows about 3–5' tall with small, hairy, gray green leaves. Nitrogen-fixing root bacteria coat the Bitterbrush's deep roots to help sustain the plants in nitrogen deficient soils. See p. 126. Their small, creamy yellow flowers bloom profusely and are followed by red

Staining Collomia

Greenleaf Manzanita

Mountain Sagebrush

Bitterbrush

Tent Caterpillars

Utah Serviceberry

fruit that nurtures tiny seeds. In spring, you may see large, grayish white "webs" created by Tent Caterpillars covering the leaves and stems of both Bitterbrush and the currants. The web covering helps the caterpillars regulate their body temperatures and protects them from predators while they consume the leaves, before they change into cocoons and later emerge as moths.

Bitterbrush seeds are consumed by chipmunks, mice, and other small animals, who cache some to eat later. If they don't return, the seeds germinate to form dense areas of new plants. The tiny Harvester Ant carries Bitterbrush seeds off to store in its nest, after consuming an enticing drop of oil in an appendage on each seed. Native Americans used the leaves as a poultice to relieve insect bites and as a tea for colds. Mothers gathered the shredded bark from older trunks and hand-softened it to make soft, absorbent diapers for their babies.

Utah Serviceberry (*Amelanchier utahensis*) is another shrub that grows 5–7' tall along the creek. Its twisted, white petals stand out against its green, serrated leaves. Its stems were used by Native Americans for arrows, and its bluish black fruits were eaten raw or left to dry in the sun to eat later.

Trailside Beaver Ponds

At dusk or under a full moon, Beavers can be seen swimming in Sagehen Creek in a pond by their dam. Beavers are peaceful, sociable animals that were almost wiped out in the fur trade and are still being killed as "varmits" by those who believe that beavers destroy habitats. Actually the opposite is true, because they play a vital role in sustaining habitats for other animals and plants by creating meadows, seep gardens, and winding creeks and tributaries that feed wetland areas. They are beneficial in so many other ways that they are now considered a vital part of habitat restoration and preservation in North America.

Since Beavers don't hibernate, all year long they cut down aspens and willows to consume their bark and to build their mud and stick dams. They also gather aspen leaves and twigs to both consume and line the floors of their lodges. In summer, they also eat grasses, ferns, and water plants. Their large 5' or-more-wide lodges are entered through one or more hidden, underwater entrances. Four to five kits are born in early spring and are 5–6" long at birth. Born with their eyes wide open and bodies fully covered with fur, they can dive into the lodge waters within 24 hours and become capable swimmers within a week. Beavers are monogamous and create affectionate families as they jointly care for their young. These sociable animals even share their dens with mice and other small animals during the winter.

Continuing On to the Big Meadow

The trail continues through aspens, conifers, and dry slopes, and within about 2 miles, it arrives at a small meadow with a tiny creek lined with pink Sierra Shooting Stars (*Dodecatheon jeffreyi*). Their 4–5 petalled nodding flowers are unusual and are one of Tahoe's many treasures. In the grasses, white Bistort grows by tiny pink to white Graceful Phlox (*Microsteris gracilis*) that nestle in the grasses. The trail then veers to the right as Stampede Reservoir, Sagehen Creek, and huge, spectacular Sagehen Meadow come into view. Right after crossing Sagehen Creek on wooden planks. look by the trail's end for the velvety, pink flowers of Hairy Paintbrush, which grow in the grasses by the Willows. At the resevoir's edge, the uncommon, white flowers of Dwarf Chamaesaracha (*Chamaesaracha nana*) bloom with a yellow central spot, low to the ground above ground carpeting leaves. While you're by the flowers, you might hear the distressed calls of a Kildeer. She may even act like she has a broken wing in her desperate effort to distract you away from her nest, which is built on the ground and sometimes near water. In past years, I have also seen large White Pelicans rest along the shoreline just enjoying the view.

Sierra Shooting Star

Graceful Phlox

Dwarf Chamaesaracha

Sagehen's Big Meadow of Camas Lilies

As you enter the big meadow in mid May after a year of good snow, you'll see an expanse of the blue to purplish flowers of the **Quamash Camas Lily**. The Washoes arrived from western Nevada each spring until the 1920s, to gather their bulbs, which they relished after roasting them in earthen ovens. See p. 213. Indigenous people have summered here for at least 4,000 years. This meadow offers such peace, that a whole day could be spent enjoying its wildflowers from the early blooming buttercups and shooting stars to later bistorts, penstemons, and onions. You'll also find the rare Plumas Ivesia (*Ivesia sericoleuca*) that carpets the ground with spreading stems of densely-packed, tiny, hairy leaflets. This Rose Family plant is only known to grow in the Northern Sierra and the Modoc Plateau.

Quamash Camas Lily

Plumas Ivesia

Nancy Gilbert

The meadow is also full of bird life. Bluebirds are often seen zipping through the meadow as bright blue streaks of delight as they catch insects on the wing. Canada Geese spend the summer raising their young and grazing on the meadow's abundant grasses and seeds. Some biologists claim that animals don't play, but of course they do. I once watched a Canada Geese pair playing on a neighbor's boathouse roof at Lake Tahoe. One would sit in the water, while the other would fly up to the top of the steeply pitched roof. After sitting for a moment to make sure its mate was watching, he or she would joyfully slide down into the water. They took turns for probably half an hour, before flying off to find some other fun place.

Common Merganser

The Common Merganzer, a duck with a "blow-dried hairdo," likes to play in the creek. A few years ago, I watched a pair of Merganzers floating and bobbing down the creek, only to fly back up it to ride down again, over and over. Mergansers dive under water to forage for fish, insects, and aquatic plants. They nest near streams in tree cavities or rock crevices and take their ducklings to the water within a day or two after hatching.

Botanists at the Sagehen Field Station have studied and appreciated the flowers at Sagehen ever since it was co-founded in 1951 with a Forest

Sagehen Creek in winter

Service user permit by Aldo Leopold's son, Starker Leopold. Aldo Leopold (1887–1948) was the author of the environmental classic, *A Sand County Almanac*, which was published after his death in 1949. Aldo would have loved Sagehen, for he once wrote, "Like winds and sunsets, wild things were taken for granted, until progress began to do away with them. Now we face the question of whether a still higher standard of living is worth its cost in things natural, wild, and free. For us of the minority, the opportunity to see geese is more important than television, and the chance to find a pasque-flower is a right as inalienable as free speech."

Leopold saw how "progress" was destroying what humans needed most . . . a deep, close bond with the natural world. I once wandered off by myself in Sagehen's meadow and happened to stop by a flower that caught my attention, as it seemed to call out to me. As I gazed down into its tiny pink blossom, I became very still and felt held in the flower's loving embrace. In those few moments, I knew deep in my heart that I am only one of many tiny beings floating on the sea of life . . . a sea made up of all other beings who will also pass on to merge with this mysterious and loving sea of energy that created this little flower, each of us, and all of nature. Somehow I knew that dying is only a transformation, not a death as we see it. This deep knowing only lasted for a few moments, but its powerful, comforting message continues to sustain me.

#9 Mount Rose

Lake Tahoe from Mt. Rose Summit

One Way: 4.8 miles
Trail Begins/Ends: 8,911'/10,778'
Map: AM: Lake Tahoe Basin
Wildflower Season: June through August

Mount Rose at 10,778' is one of only three peaks at Tahoe above 10,000' to experience the excitement of being on a mountain top in a true alpine environment. The trailhead begins along rock stewn slopes of colorful Sulphur Flowers and penstemons. After passing sun filled, forested gardens of flowers, the trail arrives at a picturesque waterfall. Creekside flowers and meadow gardens lead toward the strenuous climb up to the summit, where you'll be rewarded with magnificent vistas of distant mountain ranges and the blue waters of Lake Tahoe. The added thrill is seeing the small, flowery gems that hunker down on the rocky slopes near the mountain's top.

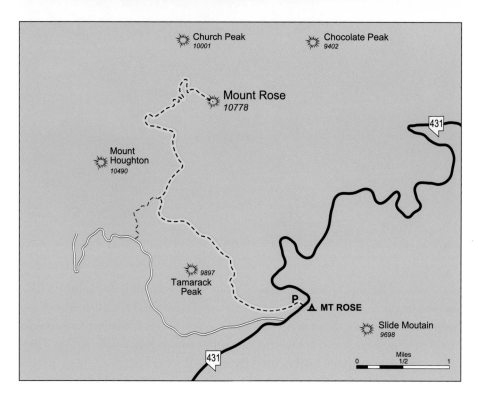

Featured Flowers

Sulphur Flower (*Eriogonum umbellatum*)

Brewer's Lupine (*Lupinus breweri*)

Showy Polemonium (*Polemonium pulcherrimum*)

Comb Draba (*Draba oligosperma*)

Cut-leaf Fleabane (*Erigeron compositus*)

Alpine Gold (*Hulsea algida*)

Trailhead Directions: **From Highway 28, near Incline Village,** turn onto Mt. Rose Highway 431 and drive 8 miles up to the Mount Rose Summit and trailhead parking by the interpretive panels. The turn-off is just past Tahoe Meadows and the excellent Forest Service Mt. Rose Campground. (Mt. and Mount are used interchangeably.) **From Reno on Highway 395,** take the Mount Rose Highway west up to the summit. Carry a warm jacket, gloves, and a warm hat; heavy, cold winds are frequent on the mountaintop, even in summer.

The trail begins along bouldered slopes and among Lodgepole and White-bark Pines. Sagebrush and Pinemat Manzanita are interspersed with blue lupines, yellow Mule's Ears, and yellow Balsamroots. In the first mile, there

Sulphur Flowers along the trail

are views of Tahoe Meadows, Lake Tahoe, and Incline Lake below. Wildflowers begin blooming along the trail in June with the 18″ tall shrubs of the **Sulphur Flower** with its intense, yellow flowers. Its blossoms lack petals but attract pollinators with their bright yellow sepals that mimic petals. They grow in umbel-shaped clusters directly above a whorl of green, leafy bracts on long, naked stems. They are abundant plants that create cheery expanses of yellow on Tahoe's mountain slopes. Indians gathered their small seeds and ground them into a flour. They also used the flowers for an eye wash and made a tea out of the roots to soothe colds. Sulphur Flower is attractive in drought tolerant gardens for its flower color, compact growth, and long blooming period. Seventeen native varieties of this plant grow throughout California, with 10 varieties in the Sierra Nevada.

Another showy plant is the 4–5′ tall Brewer's Angelica (*Angelica breweri*), which is in the Umbel Family. This family can be identified by its tiny,

white flowers that grow in round clusters on stems that radiate outward from a single point on the main stem, like the spokes of an umbrella. Its large leaves are pinnate and widely lance-shaped with serrated leaflets. If you gently scratch the stem, you'll be able to inhale its lovely fragrance. A similar though smaller member of the same family is Gray's Lovage (*Ligusticum grayii*). It grows nearby up to 2½′ tall with finely divided, pinnate leaves and smaller, white flower clusters.

Brewer's Angelica

You'll also find the 1–3' tall Tahoe Lupine (*Lupinus argenteus* var. *meionanthus*) found at elevations above 8,000'. Its silvery, palmate leaves and blue, rounded pea flowers have a yellow banner spot. The 18" tall Mountain Pennyroyal (*Monardella odoratissima*) prefers the same habitat and has clusters of white to lavender flowers that give off a strong mint fragrance as the air volatizes the oils in their leaves. A funny, little, yellow flowered plant, Shaggy Hawkweed (*Hieracium horridum*), is very fuzzy like a shaggy sweater, and its disk flowers are held in fuzzy, hairy phyllaries. "Horridum" isn't for horrible; it's just Latin for "hairy."

Gray's Lovage

Getting Acquainted with Penstemons

Penstemons are some of Tahoe's prettiest flowers in dry, rocky habitats. The Showy Penstemon (*Penstemon speciosus*) begins blooming early in June, with inch long flowers and flaring petals above a tube that bulges in the middle like a tiny beer belly. Its leaves are leathery, up to 3" long, and folded lengthwise. All penstemons have 5 stamens, but one of them is a staminode, which is a stamen without an anther. "Penstemon" is from the Greek "pente" for "five" and "stemon" for "stamen." To identify these flowers by species, you'll need to find the staminode. Look into the flower, and you'll see two thread-

Tahoe Lupine

like structures: one will be the staminode without an anther and the other will be the style attached to an ovary. A hand lens helps to see if the staminode is hairy or bald, which is important in keying out penstemons.

Looking at this detail will draw you into the beauty of these flowers. Mountain Pride (*Penstemon newberryi*) grows with bright pink flowers in the same dry habitats. Its sparsely hairy staminode and white woolly anthers

Shaggy Hawkweed

Roger Rosenberger

Showy Penstemon

Mountain Pride

Azure Penstemon

peek out from the throat. See if you can also find the style; how does it differ from the staminode? The style rises directly out of the ovary, the filament does not; it grows like the other stamens. The Azure Penstemon (*Penstemon azureus*) has yellow buds and blue violet flowers. Is its staminode hairy or bald? As the trail enters the forest, you'll find the Slender Penstemon (*Penstemon gracilentus*), which grows about 18″ tall with blue, narrow tubed, glandular flowers. Can you find its staminode? It's hairy and resembles a tiny toothbrush, which a mouse or little beetle might use! Check it out, it's really cute.

Through the Forest

As the trail climbs uphill toward the eastern side of Tamarack Peak, you'll pass carpets of **Brewer's Lupine**, a low-growing perennial with blue flowers and a yellow or white spot on the upper banner petal. It grows 3–5″ tall and like other lupines, it can live in nitrogen deficient soils. Nitrogen fixing bacteria on its roots convert nitrogen in the air of the soil into a form the plant can use. When the plant dies it decomposes and releases the nitrogen into the soil to nurture other plants. You'll also find Shasta Knotweed (*Polygonum shastense*), a low growing shrub that was first collected in northern California on Mount Shasta. Its inch long leaves are rolled under along the edges, and its woody stems support small, white flowers with dark mid-veins.

Slender Penstemon

Brewer's Lupine

While in the forest, you may be treated to the lilting song of a Mountain Chickadee. In my early days of hiking, its sweet song welcomed me to the mountains; it was only later that I learned who sang with such joy. Chickadees flit from tree to tree searching for insects and can be seen hanging upside down as they forage. They split open Lodgepole Pine needles to eat the tiny larvae of Needle-miner Moths. In April and May, chickadees mate and select their territory and

Shasta Knotweed

begin building nests in tree cavities made by woodpeckers. As the female incubates the eggs, she is fed faithfully by the male. Chickadees are one of the few birds that remain in the woods throughout the winter, seeming to enjoy stormy days as happily as they do sunny ones. Tom Brown, an experienced tracker, once asked his Apache teacher, Stalking Wolf, to name his favorite animal. Instead of choosing a soaring eagle or a powerful bear, Stalking Wolf chose

Mountain Chickadee

the chickadee, because as he said, "It is cheerful like a ray of sunshine in the darkest of storms and can be a symbol for us to radiate our strengths, even when the moment may seem bleak."

Arriving at Galena Creek

Soon, you'll begin a gradual descent and cross a seasonal stream and within 2.3 miles from the trailhead, you'll reach Galena Creek's lovely waterfall. It cascades over a wide, rock-strewn wall down past Large-leaf Lupines and Alpine Sageworts (*Artemisia noregica*). Sageworts prefer high elevation habitats and grow up to 3' tall with pinnate leaves and nod-ding, yellow flowers with black-edged phyllaries. As you sit by the falls, you

Galena Creek's Falls

may be visited by a Golden-mantled Ground Squirrel, looking for delicious morsels dropped by hikers.

From the falls, it is about 2.5 miles to the top of Mount Rose, which is well worth the climb for those in good shape and acclimated to the high elevation. If you planned to hike just to the

Alpine Sagewort

Golden-mantled Ground Squirrel

Red Elderberry

falls, a nice side-trip is to hike up the trail on the left side of the falls to explore upper Galena Creek and the wet meadows and pond along the old Mount Rose Trail. If you do so, look for the white flowers of the Alpine Gentian (*Gentiana newberryi*), which are scattered in the grasses and on open ground near a pond.

To continue toward the summit of Mount Rose, follow the main trail from the falls along the rocky hillside by Galena Creek. Look up in rocks just past the falls for the shrubs of the Red Elderberry (*Sambucus racemosa* var. *racemosa*). All parts of this plant are poisonous, though cooking removes the toxicity. It grows up to about 4' tall with clusters of white to creamy flowers that are followed by bright red fruit. Blue Elderberries (*Sambucus nigra* var. *caerulea*) are also found at Tahoe, but are less common. They can be cooked to make a sweet syrup, jams and even processed for wine. If you scratch the leaves of Elderberry plants, they smell like burnt peanut butter. "Sambucus" is Greek for "musical instrument." As they have for generations, Native Americans still create flutes and clapper sticks from the larger stems of Elderberries.

As you wander along the trail, in grassy areas right by the creek, look for white Macloskey's Violets and yellow Plantain Buttercups carpeting the ground by taller plants of Lewis' Monkeyflowers, Alpine Lilies, and willows.

Barren Slopes of Whitebark Pine

Heading up to the Summit

After crossing several creeks, you'll pass a junction with the old Mount Rose Trail. At this point you'll cross a tributary of Galena Creek and begin climbing up a narrow canyon. After crossing more seasonal creeks, you'll arrive at the wilderness boundary and junction for Big Meadows and Mount Rose. The trail heads right and climbs along a narrow ridge past rugged, twisted Whitebark Pines and then reaches open, rock-strewn slopes. As you climb above the tree-line on a series of switchbacks, dramatic views appear. The alpine flowers above the tree-line usually begin blooming in early June. In one visit, you won't see all the flowers I mention, because each plant has its own brief time to flower before going to seed and drying up. One plant with the longest blooming period is the Alpine Paintbrush (*Castilleja nana*), which we've seen on our other hikes, but here you'll find it with bracts in another color variation.

Alpine Paintbrush

One of the cutest flowers this high on the mountain is the Mount Rose Wild Buckwheat (*Eriogonum rosense*), which was first discovered on Mount Rose. It only grows 3–6" tall but is

Mount Rose Wild Buckwheat

Showy Polemonium

Comb Draba

Cut-leaf Fleabane

Alpine Buttercup

so colorful you can't miss its yellow flowers when in bloom. You'll also find the **Showy Polemonium** (*Polemonium pulcherrimum*), which is usually abundant here, because it prefers altitudes above 8,000'. Its purple to bluish, bowl-shaped flowers bloom above tiny, oval leaflets that grow pinnately and densely along the stems.

The bright yellow **Comb Draba** is a cheery little plant that prefers exposed hillsides. It's uncommon, so it is a special treat to see it here. Also look for the sweet, white to pink daisy flowers of the **Cut-leaf Fleabane**. It grows 2–6" tall with densely haired leaves. Another favorite is the Alpine Buttercup (*Ranunculus eschscholtzii*). It colors the slopes with golden, shiny-petaled flowers with friendly little faces that seem delighted to be in such a harsh habitat.

On the final climb before the very top, the wind may feel as if it could blow you right off the mountain. It also feels like a place where there should be Tibetan prayer flags flapping in the wind! The exhilarating air and the fragile, beautiful world of brightly colored plants is a treasure that few people ever experience.

Most alpine plants have adapted to such habitats with their minimal water, fierce winds, and intense sunlight by growing compactly and covering themselves with insulating, white hairs, and the Cushion Phlox (*Phlox condensata*) is so compact that it's impossible to penetrate its leaves, even with pressure from a finger. This helps it to resist the violent winds that could tear or desiccate its leaves, and it also helps retain precious heat during cold nights. Studies have shown that nighttime temperatures inside such dense mats can be as much as 20 degrees warmer than the outside air.

Nature teaches us that there are many different ways to evolve and adapt to various environments and challenges. Beautiful **Alpine Gold** grows here above the tree-line, but it doesn't hunker down as do the cushion plants. It grows 4–12″ tall with 4″ long, hairy leaves and golden, 2½″ wide flowers. It has adapted to live here with a bold determination that defies the odds by growing so tall, and yet it survives just fine protected by its insulating, hairy leaves.

Cushion Phlox

The final gift at the summit are the Showy Polemoniums that are tucked down in the rocks. Though they are found earlier on the hike, it's amazing to find them at the very top, because they seem so tender and vunerable here on the summit. John Muir appreciated alpine plants as ". . . gentle mountaineers face to face with the sky, kept safe and warm by a thousand miracles, seeming always the finer and purer the wilder and stormier their homes."

It's important to realize that alpine plants above the tree-line have only a few months or in some cases just a few weeks to bloom, spread, and set seed. Most alpine plants are perennials that put on very little growth in a year.

Alpine Gold

A short, thick, bonsai-like stem means the plant has been growing for a very long time. Staying on the trail will help protect the plants, because a rock accidentally kicked and dislodged can destroy a plant that may have been struggling to survive for 100 years or more.

Arriving at the Summit

Upon arriving at the summit, you'll have a 360-degree vista. On a clear day, you may even be able to see Mt. Lassen over a hundred miles to the north. I don't recommend what I'm about tell you, because sudden storms can blow in even on a clear day, but I once spent the night on the summit. It was

Sulphur Flowers along the Mount Rose Trail

magical as the stars sparkled in the darkened sky, and the moon rose and shone down on the boulders surrounding us. In the morning I awakened to a spectacular pink sunrise, but as I began moving, I was quite surprised to feel what seemed like hundreds of moths fluttering in my sleeping bag. They must have been brought to the summit by a wind current. After being deposited by the wind, they sought shelter in my down bag, which must have been a pretty luxurious way station for these little, wind-drifted adventurers.

When you are ready to head back down the mountain to return home or to camp out below, your body will probably be tired, but I think you'll be pleased with what you've experienced on this powerful mountain. If you are like me, one who likes to linger until most others have left the trails, you'll have the peaceful experience of walking out as the sun is slowly setting, spreading its golden light and long shadows across the lush, green meadows.

#10 Squaw Valley's Shirley Canyon

Squaw Valley's upper ski area in June

One Way: Approximately 2.5 miles
Trail Begins/Ends: 6,200'/8,400'
Map: AM: Lake Tahoe Basin
Wildflower Season: May through September

During spring Shirley Canyon's exuberant Squaw Creek rushes, splashes, and sings in torrents of delight, dancing over granite walls and flowing through narrow gorges—a jubilant journey that is subdued to a gentle wandering as its waters travel over broad granitic slabs or linger momentarily in quiet pools. In the canyon's icy creeks, a determined little bird swims upstream gathering delicious morsels. Seep gardens of flowers brighten the creeksides with a rainbow of color. Higher up the mountain, unusual plants of Bird's Beak and Keckiella grow on open hillsides. In fall, bright red California Fuchsias and intensely colored blue Explorer's Gentians grace rock gardens as the season comes to an end.

133

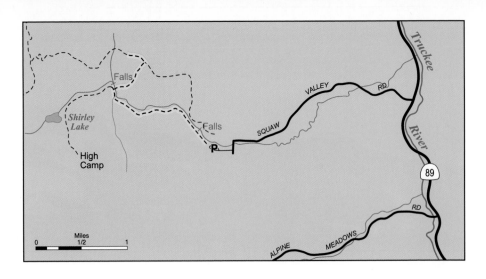

Featured Flowers

California Skullcap (*Scutellaria californica*)
Thimbleberry (*Rubus parviflorus*)
Washington Lily (*Lilium washingtonianum*)
Slender Bird's Beak (*Cordylanthus tenuis*)
Lemmon's Keckiella (*Keckiella lemmonii*)
California Fuchsia (*Epilobium canun*)

Trailhead Directions: The entrance to Squaw Valley is located between Truckee and Tahoe City on Highway 89. Take the main road along Squaw Valley's big meadow and turn left onto Squaw Peak Road. Drive over the bridge toward the ski area's gondola building. Just before the building, turn right onto Squaw Peak Way and then turn right to head through the condominiums to the trailhead and Shirley Canyon Trail sign.

The trail begins in a forest of Lodgepole Pines with the understory shrubs of Bittercherry, Tobacco Brush, and Mountain Spiraea. After a short walk, when you hear the sound of the first waterfall, take the side trail to the right to reach the falls. Look for the

Shirley Creek's first waterfall

6–12" tall plants of **California Skullcap** blooming in June near the trail junction. This Mint
Family plant lacks the usual mint fragrance, but
a tea made from the leaves is a soothing sedative. Their white flowers are 2-lipped with the
upper lip forming a hood over the reproductive
parts, and the lower, lobed lip creates a landing
pad for pollinators.

California Skullcap

Near the creek in the shade of conifers in
May or June, you'll find the large, maple-like
leaves and white flowers of **Thimbleberry**.
Later, their red fruits ripen in cup-like recepta-
cles and can be eaten as small treats. In the 1791
diary of a naturalist traveling on a ship along the
coast of America, John Meares wrote, "On the
rocky islands, and in the woods . . . is a species
of raspberry of the most delicious flavour, and
far superior to any fruit of that kind we had ever
before tasted. It grows on a larger bush than our
European raspberry, and is free of thorns; but
the fruit itself is so delicate, that a shower of rain
washes it entirely away."

Thimbleberry

In June through July in the rocks above
the creek, the tubular flowers of Mountain Pride
(*Penstemon newberryi*) add splashes of vibrant
pink, and the star-shaped flowers of Scarlet
Gilia (*Ipomopsis aggregata*), Sulphur Flower
(*Eriogonum umbellatum*), and Sierra Onion
(*Allium campanulatum*) create colorful rock gardens. The star-shaped onion flowers form identical sepals and petals that radiate outward from
a central point on a naked stem. The bulbs and
leaves were gathered by the Washoes in Shirley
Canyon to flavor their foods. The bulbs were
consumed raw or eaten after being roasted in
earthen ovens. The seeds were roasted in open
willow baskets with hot rocks and then eaten as
is or were ground and added to flavor foods.

Mountain Pride

Sierra Onion

Pink Alumroot

The delicate flowered Pink Alumroot (*Heuchera rubescens*) grows from 4–12" tall on rock ledges and out of vertical cracks in the rocks above the creek. Their roots penetrate the cracks and tenaciously hold on through the years. Its red sepals enclose teensie white to pink flowers that bloom on slender stems. Indigenous people dried and ground their astringent roots and applied the powder to open cuts to stop bleeding. The roots were also used in a soothing gargle for sore throats.

As you pass through wooded areas, look for the large flowers of the spectacular **Washington Lily**. It blooms in July on 4–5' tall stems with trumpet-shaped, white flowers that are intensely fragrant. It was named for Martha Washington and was favored by John Muir, who came across it one morning on a July day in 1869 in Yosemite, "Found the white fragrant Washington lily, the finest of all the Sierra lilies . . . A lovely flower, worth going hungry and footsore endless miles to see. The whole world seems richer now that I have found this plant in so noble a landscape."

Washington Lily

The Active Pussypaws

In open, drying areas, look for the ground carpeting leaves of Pussy Paws (*Calyptridium umbellatum*). Their spoon-shaped leaves form a green basal rosette, which means they radiate outward from the base of the flower stems.

Pussy Paws

Gently squeeze one of its white to pink flower clusters to feel their little "paws." The flower's 4 petals are papery and hard to differentiate from their papery sepals, unless they are viewed through a hand lens. Two species of Calyptridium grow at Tahoe, and since they hybridize they can have characteristics of both species, which makes it difficult to tell them apart. Generally, *C. umbellatum* has white flowers and one "pussypaw" per leafy rosette and *C. monospermum* has white to rosey pink flowers with two or more "pussy paws" per basal rosette. Also, the stems of *C. umbellatum* usually lack leaves, while the stems of the other species usually have tiny leaves.

Pussy Paws are interesting, because they have adapted to hot, dry habitats in an unusual way. Early in the morning in cool temperatures, the flowers rest on the ground, but as the day warms up, they rise up and cool themselves by breaking contact with the hot ground. This rising is caused by tension in the stems due to the heat-induced increase of water pressure in cells located where the stem is attached to the plant's base. As the day cools, and the pressure is released, the stems begin to move downward and lie flat on the cooler ground by night-time. In late summer, the soft "paws" produce tiny, black seeds that feed chipmunks and other small rodents.

A Year Round Resident

In walking along the creek past Black Cottonwoods and Quaking Aspens, keep your eyes open for the Dipper, or Water Ouzel that bobs up and down on the rocks by the creek. These birds are usually solitary, except when they pair to mate and raise their young. Their nests are made out of mossy materials and are built near rushing water or are hidden behind waterfalls. The female lays three to six white eggs in spring, and the young hatch in about two weeks. They remain in the nest for almost a month,

Nancy Gilbert

Dipper

and as soon as they fledge, they begin bobbing on the rocks by their parents. It's not known why they do this, perhaps they're just happy little birds that like to dance.

You will often spot a Dipper flying rapidly up the creek only a few inches above the surface in search of food. When it spots an insect, it quickly plunges into the water and swims submerged through the rapids, propelled by its short but powerful wings. On other occasions, it casually walks submerged along the sandy bottom of streams foraging for tasty larvae, as if taking an afternoon stroll. The Dipper lacks the webbed feet of most water birds, which is an advantage, because it allows it to effectively grip the floor of the stream under the water. Dippers are able to survive frigid, winter temperatures, because their oil glands are larger than those of most birds and provide enough oil to waterproof their feathers. Their thick, downy undercoats also help to insulate them.

John Muir described the Dipper as "a singularly joyous and lovable little fellow, about the size of a robin clad in a plain waterproof suit of bluish gray, with a tinge of chocolate on the head and shoulders . . . He is the mountain streams' own darling, the hummingbird of blooming waters, loving rocky ripple slopes and sheets of foam as a bee loves flowers, as a lark loves sunshine and meadows. Among all the mountain birds none has cheered me so much in my lonely wanderings – none so unfailingly."

Arriving at the Second Waterfall

As you continue uphill from the waterfall, you'll pass beds of Thimbleberries covering the ground under the trees, before the trail breaks out into the sun by Greenleaf Manzanitas (*Arctostaphylos patula*). Manzanitas bloom

Greenleaf Manzanita

with nectar-laden, pink, urn-shaped flowers in May or June on plants with mahogany colored bark. Look at the flowers closely to see the tiny holes made by bees that sip the nectar without pollinating the flowers. You'll also pass Pinemat Manzanitas (*A. nevadensis*) with smaller leaves but similar white flowers. It grows as a dense, ground hugging shrub. The small, sweet, red berries of all manzanitas were gathered by the Washoe and made into a refreshing drink. They were also dried and added to hot dishes or mixed with seeds, dried fruit, and meat.

Pinemat Manzanita

Pinemat Manzanita fruit

The second waterfall is soon reached by large granitic slabs just as the trail turns left to head up to Shirley Lake, which could be a hike for another day. The canyon and the lake were named for Shirley Houghton, who with his father C. S. Houghton and other pals used to make annual trips into this once remote area to enjoy the isolation, beauty, and great fishing. Their trips began in the late 1800s and continued through several generations. Shirley Houghton was usually the first to reach the lake and would be in the water by the time the others arrived. This tradition was continued by C. S. Houghton's grandson, Winslow Hall, who related the story to me. After hiking up to Shirley Lake and taking a swim, they headed down into the Five Lakes Basin to Hell Hole. There the fishing was reported to be so good that they would waken each morning, and standing up in their sleeping bags, they would cast a line and catch a trout on each cast for breakfast. Since they were fishermen, can we really believe this story? Maybe, but regardless, it's a charming story!

Continuing up the Canyon

After this waterfall, walk up to a third gorgeous waterfall and then back-track down the trail to find a place to cross over the creek and pick up another trail. On this side of the creek, you'll find Crimson

Seep-spring Monkeyflower

Columbines, ferns, and Seep-spring Monkeyflowers (*Mimulus guttatus*). Indians ate the young monkeyflower leaves and stems raw or mashed them into a poultice to apply to burns or insect bites for pain relief.

Whisker Brush

Along the trail in drying habitats, you'll find cute, lit-tle Whisker Brush flowers (*Leptosiphon ciliatus*). Its plants grow up to 4" tall with ⅜" wide, pink flowers. Its densely whorled, whisker-brush-like leaves are hairy and needle-shaped. This is a "must see" plant with a hand lens. Continue up the trail looking for the Bear Buckwheat (*Eriogonum ursinum*). Its creamy flowers grow in tight clus-ters on top of 6–18" tall, naked stems above small, woolly leaves that form mats in dry habitats.

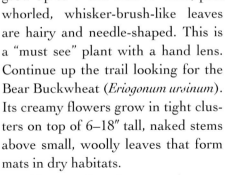
Bear Buckwheat

Many trails criss-cross the can-yon, so when you arrive at a trail that heads east, follow it and continue up the canyon as the trail heads north. After crossing another creek, you'll climb up through open, volcanic slopes covered in July with Mule's Ears, Balsamroots, and lavender flowered Spurred Lupines. In drier, open areas, be on the lookout for two

Lupine and Mule's Ears meadow

Slender Bird's Beak

Lemmon's Keckiella shrub

Lemmon's Keckiella flower

California Fuchsia

uncommon plants. **Slender Bird's Beak** is aptly named for its strange flowers that form two lips like a bird's beak. It grows from 1–3′ tall with white flowers that are yellow-tipped and spotted with maroon to purple. This annual is a root parasite that puts out haustoria to absorb water and nutrients from nearby host plants. **Lemmon's Keckiella** blooms in similar habitats with yellow flowers on loosely growing plants up to 5′ tall. Its ½″ long flowers are lovely through a hand lens. The 2 upper petals are brownish purple and nectar lines mark the lower petals. Four stamens form an arch below the upper petals guiding insects into the flower's secret chamber and to their nectaries.

Red Fuchsias Decorate the Rocks

After large slopes of Mule's Ears and Balsamroots, the trail climbs up to granite slabs high on the mountainside, and then heads west with wonderful views of Squaw Valley's meadow. This large, beautiful meadow was a popular summer home for the Washoe people. Trout were abundant in the creeks, and the canyon was rich with game and plant foods. When explorers first entered the meadow, they found only Washoe women and children, because the men were out hunting, so the explorers named it Squaw Valley. We now know that "squaw" was a degrading name applied to women by crass explorers. Based on this, "squaw" for old plant names, like Squaw Carpet, is no longer used.

In August to September among the rocks, you'll find the **California Fuchsia**. Its red, flashy flowers bloom above soft, hairy leaves, and its red reproductive parts extend enticingly outward from the flaring petals. Fuchsias provide vital nectar for south migrating hummingbirds later in the season, when most other wildflowers have withered and gone to seed. Native Americans made a tea from its leaves to help relieve general kidney problems, and a blue dye was made from its roots.

Another late bloomer in the canyon is the vivid blue Explorer's Gentian (*Gentiana calycosa*). Look for it in the forest on the north side creek down by the first waterfall in damp areas. If you are in this same area in May, look for the unusual flowers of Steer's Head (*Dicentra uniflora*) that carpet the ground with gray green leaves. Its white to pink flowers bloom soon after the snow melts.

Explorer's Gentian

Shirley Canyon is a special place anytime, but it is especially special in a wild rainstorm or during a light snowfall. When the weather looks rainy, it's comfortable to stay inside with a good book by the fire, yet this can be one of the most exciting times to be out. On sunny days the trees, flowers, and animals bask lazily in the sun's warmth or busily go about their business of food gathering and living. But in a storm, something else happens. The swaying trees and branches dance in wild abandon, and an intense energy permeates the forest. Once in a windy snowstorm in Shirley Canyon, I decided to bundle up and leave my warm house to head up the canyon. I was surprised to see that the birds were not huddled in the trees, as I would have expected. They were wildly flying up and down the canyon, deliriously excited by the storm's energy. Huge conifers, cottonwoods, and aspens swayed back and forth in the wind with the excited birds taking no notice of me in their delight.

So I faded into the background to watch the grand show as the trees and birds let loose with a frenzied abandon to express their joy. I wanted to join them and be unobtrusive, so I stretched out on a large, flat rock letting the soggy snow fall down upon me. Since I was dressed for the storm, I never felt the cold, only the exuberance of wet snow falling upon my face, and the wind wildly swirling around me. I hadn't realized it before, but until that moment, I had sometimes felt like a visitor in the forest, but on this day I felt welcomed and grateful to be included in the celebration. So don't stay home if the weather is stormy; instead, bundle up and head out into this beautiful canyon to see what you might find!

#11 Page Meadows

Parish's Yampa covers the meadow
Geoff Griffin

🥾 to 🥾🥾

One Way: 0.5 to 2+ miles
Trail Begins/Ends: 6,600′
Map: AM: Lake Tahoe Basin
Wildflower Season: June through August

Page Meadows is a series of large, meandering, sun-filled meadows between forests of conifers and aspens. In June they come alive with butter-cups and camas lilies and later with lacey yampahs and purple penstemons. The meadows are a popular place for locals, but still retain an isolated, peaceful feeling. Children can experience butterflies pollinating flowers and Chorus Frogs hopping among tiny, blue Porterellas. As summer turns into fall, flowers and grasses go to seed, welcoming bird life. Aspen leaves turn golden and flutter in the afternoon breezes. Winter brings cross-country skiing and snow-shoeing through flat expanses of snow with the thrilling possibility of seeing a coyote moving with a rhythmic gait through the white, blanketed landscape.

142

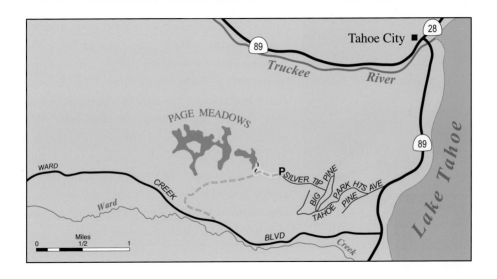

Featured Flowers
Anderson's Thistle (*Cirsium andersonii*)
Parish's Yampah (*Perideridia parishii*)
Alpine Aster (*Oreostemma alpigenum*)
Porterella (*Porterella carnosula*)
Canada Goldenrod (*Solidago elongata*)
Torrey's Blue-eyed Mary (*Collinsia torreyi*)

Trailhead directions: **From Tahoe City** on Highway 89, drive south 1.9 miles and take a right onto Pine Avenue. **From South Lake Tahoe**, drive about 24.7 miles north on Hwy 89, and turn left onto Pine Avenue. Head uphill 0.1 mile and turn right onto Tahoe Park Heights for 0.6 mile to a three way split. Take Big Pine 0.2 mile straight head and turn left onto Silver Tip Drive for 0.4 mile to the parking area where the road ends at the unsigned trailhead.

The unsigned trail begins in a forest of Jeffrey and Lodgepole Pines and White Firs, with an understory of Bittercherry, Whitethorn, and Pinemat Manzanita, and it shortly arrives at a large opening, where you'll veer left onto an old dirt road that is level and an easy walk for children. Look for Sticky Cinquefoils, Scarlet

Page Meadows is for youngsters too

Anderson's
Thistle &
Western Tiger
Swallowtail

The Thistle's tiny
seed drifts away

Parish's Yampah

Geoff Griffin

Gilias, White-veined Mallows, and **Anderson's Thistle**, which grows up to 3½' tall. Its pink disk flowers are tightly clustered in overlapping, leafy, thorn-tipped phyllaries. After pollination, the flower's pappus opens into fluffy "parachutes" to distribute the mature seeds in the wind. Within a half mile, and with no trail sign, there will be two 3' tall posts on the right by a trail that leads down to the first meadow. From that meadow you can wander through all the various meadows that are linked up through the trees.

In June, Plantain Buttercups, Quamash Camas Lilies, Elephant's Heads, and Alpine Shooting Stars bloom, followed in July by yellow Primrose Monkeyflowers, white Bistorts, and yellow Arrowleaf Butterweeds. In some years, the meadows are covered with lacey, white-flowered **Parish's Yampah**. Its umbel flowers are either staminate or bisexual, and its leaves are pinnate with 1–3 pairs of linear leaflets. Their sweet tuberous roots were an important food for all California Indians who roasted them in earthen ovens or ate them raw, and its caraway-flavored seeds were also consumed. Meadow Penstemons (*Penstemon rydbergii*) create waves of blue purple in a good year, after the camas lilies have gone to seed. **Alpine Asters** decorate the meadows with daisy-like, lavender flowers that bloom above densely hairy phyllaries on solitary stems. After entering the meadow, you can wander through it or take the trail off to the right. The trail soon returns to the meadow on a waffle-path and continues into an upper meadow and to the meadows beyond.

Alpine Aster

A Meadow's Complex Community

Meadows are full of life even though they may seem like quiet places without much "happening," except perhaps for the lilting songs of Red-wing Blackbirds or the buzzing of mosquitoes. If we could see through the grasses and down into the soil, and if our ears could pick up the subtle underground noises, we would be amazed at the abundant life. Thousands of invertebrates live among the grasses in various stages of maturity from larvae to adult, and unknown numbers of bacteria and soil fungi live in the soils forming communities that sustain the lives of trees and other plants. Pollinating insects circulate through and above the grasses feeding on pollen and nectar.

Voles form narrow, underground tunnels and above ground pathways through the grasses as they forage for food. Moles spend their entire lives underground in a network of tunnels. They don't have external ears, but

they have superior hearing and can find prey under the ground by listening for movements that resonate through the soil. Meadow mice scamper through the grasses foraging for seeds and herbs, before returning to their underground burrows to store food, sleep, mate, and rear their young.

If you explore the first meadow in June, you'll find small "vernal" pools, created from depressions that catch the spring snowmelt. Chorus Frogs live in the pools and sing their little hearts out as evening approaches by inflating their throat pouches in romantic displays for females. They are only 1–2″ long and live in ponds even at 11,000′ elevations. The female lays eggs in the summer in a mass of soft, sticky jelly, which adheres to the blades and stems of water plants. Tadpoles emerge in summer and live in the pools until they transform into frogs.

As the water in the shallow ponds recedes, small "belly plants" begin carpeting the boggy soil. One of the prettiest is **Porterella**. It's an annual that grows only a few inches tall, but it is impressive when it blooms abundantly. You'll also see

Nancy Gilbert

Chorus Frog

Porterellas bloom in shallow pools

Needle Navarretia

Mitten-leaf Nemophila

Nancy Gilbert

Coyotes hunt in the meadow

Mule Deer

other flowers in the drying soil. The Needle Navarretia (*Navarretia minima*) has tiny, ¼″ wide, white flowers above needle-like leaves, and the white or bluish flowers of the small Mitten-leaf Nemophila (*Nemophila spatulata*) bloom among their mitten-shaped leaves.

Other Creatures in the Meadows

At the meadow's edge, you may spot a cute Belding's Ground Squirrel sitting up by its burrow. See p. 235. Snowshoe Hares forage in the meadow grasses but are rarely seen, because they usually sleep during the day and graze from dusk to dawn. Since they don't hibernate, they adapt to winter with thickened fur that turns white to blend with the snow. Animals like these are what draw Coyotes to hunt in the meadow.

Coyotes are clever, adaptable omnivores and excellent hunters, who are able to change their breeding habitats in response to environmental changes and so have been successful in spite of human invasion into their habitats. They live in dens and give birth to their young in spring.

You may see Mule Deer grazing in the meadow in late afternoon, as the sun spreads its golden light across the grasses. Fawns are born in late spring or summer. If you find one in the bushes, the mother is probably out grazing to sustain her milk, so don't approach it. Fawns know to stay still, if something approaches. Most deer migrate to lower elevations, as winter snows cover their browsing shrubs.

Meadows and other natural habitats sustain many lives but are also important for many other reasons. Healthy meadows, range-lands, and forests cover immense areas of the earth and by photosynthesis produce oxygen. Plants reduce erosion by holding topsoil in place. They store water through root uptake, and evaporate it off their leaves returning it to the soil beneath them. They buffer intense weather and purify water as it moves through the soil. They are also an important, natural way to respond to global warming as they remove carbon from the air and sequester it in the soil in immense, measureable amounts. Natural, healthy plant communities are more resilient than our vast, agricultural, human-produced monocultures. Because natural plant communities are so diverse, if their vast areas are left intact, they will be more able to adapt as the planet heats up and thereby be more able to provide a life support system.

Miniature Tarweed

Drying Environments

Look for tiny, pink flowers of ground-carpeting Ruby Sand Spurry (*Spergularia rubra*). See p. 36. You'll also find the tiny-flowered 1–5" tall Miniature Tarweed (*Hemizonella minima*) with its 3–5 yellow ray flowers and 1–2 disk flowers. Canada Goldenrod (*solidago elongata*) is a late bloomer with numerous golden, daisy-like flowers on 1–3' tall stems. Native Americans chewed the flowers to help heal a sore throat and used its fluffy pappus as tinder for fire starting. Look for white foam on the stems of goldenrods created by tiny, green, wingless Spittlebug nymphs. They harmlessly attach themselves to herbaceous plant stems to suck their juices with their needle-like mouth parts. As they pump their bodies, they create frothy bubbles in which they hide for protection from predators. The froth keeps their bodies moist, and it also insulates them from heat and cold. As they mature, they become brown or black Spittlebugs.

Canada Goldenrod

Nymph's froth

Creeping Snowberry

Torrey's Blue-eyed Mary

Pinewoods Lousewort

In forested areas, you'll find Creeping Snowberry (*Symphoricarpos mollis*). It is a low growing shrub with arching stems. Tiny, pink, bell-shaped flowers hang down, followed by berries white as snow. You'll also find **Torrey's Blue-eyed Mary** with tiny ½″ flowers on its 2–10″ long stems. Its flowers delicately cover large areas under the trees and are best viewed through a hand lens to appreciate their beauty. You'll also find the Pinewoods Lousewort (*Pedicularis semibarbata*) that grows low to the ground with small yellow flowers and leaves that resemble ferns. Its odd name is from an old belief that domestic animals would eliminate their lice, if they grazed on these plants.

Sharing the Meadows with Children

Recently, I was in the first meadow and was delighted to see a group of young children running freely through the grasses and flowers with great joy. There are many ways to experience these meadows. Time outdoors with our children will be especially meaningful, if they feel free to run and wander, and if we enter their world by sharing what interests them most. As we all know, children have a natural ability to connect with plants in a way that most adults have forgotten, but we can re-remember this connection.

Students in my classes often ask me how Indians knew which plants were safe to eat or use as medicine. I respond that I'm sure in the very beginning they must have learned some things by trial and error and by watching what the animals ate. In time this was passed on by the Elders, and Indians tell us that their ancestors were so intimately involved with plants that they communicated directly with them.

Some still do as they honor and appreciate plants for food and medicines.

When I share this, a few skeptics roll their eyes. I understand their skepticism, but when I invite them to find out what they might experience during my class, most become intrigued by the possibility. Michael Hutton, who writes about listening to the land in *The Wisdom of Listening*, says of trees "we need to give them our full attention. The ways they speak to us are subtle. We can listen with our ears, but in another way, we must listen with our hearts as well; we must listen with our whole bodies. When we listen this way, we are immediately rewarded . . . Interestingly, there are indigenous people who claim they can hear the voice of the tree spirits. So, if these people can hear the trees, why can't the rest of us?" We can!

A subtle communication

Giving plants our full attention with respect and love is how we begin. I came into the world loving plants, but true listening began for me after spending many hours and days alone in nature. From my home in Tahoe, I could walk out my back door into wild forests and creekside meadows. Sometimes as I wandered I would stop, find a "nest" under a tree, and fall asleep. When I awakened my mind was quiet, which helped me to be more present with all that was around me. I then began to *see* plants in a deeper way, instead of just looking *at* them. Through this, I began to learn from plants very meaningful, personal insights for my own life.

Communicating with Plants

Such insights helped me to realize that all living beings are amazing expressions of the life force and that we all belong to the same earth community. Though plants compete for resources with other plants and animals just as people do, they also cooperate and adapt to stresses through many mutually beneficial relationships with other plants,

Phlox and Paintbrush "pals"

insects, soil fungi, and even bacteria. This encouraged me to express and value what was unique in me . . . my deep connection with plants and all of Nature.

After spending solitary time in the meadows and woods, I felt peaceful being alone and began to rest held in the "arms" of Nature. In time, trust developed, and I began to see the natural world as a vast, wise community that had much to teach me. Slowly I began to communicate with plants, first through just sensing them more deeply, as gardeners do who love plants. After several years of greeting them with gratitude, I began to naturally communicate with them, and finally with some apprehension, I began sharing my way of doing so in some of my classes.

After sharing my process of communication with adults, children, and teenagers, most returned to the class group with affirming stories, like an 8-year-old who told me, "You taught me an important lesson. You taught me I can talk to flowers through my feelings. I think this has changed my life forever." Another 8-year-old told me that she was hyper and could never sit still, but when she sat down with the plant that had chosen her, she became quiet inside. She said her plant assured her that she could return to it whenever she needed to feel calm. Children love plants and are open to communicating with them, before they are talked out of it later in life. Nothing is more powerful in the Universe than love. George Washington Carver, who loved flowers and spoke with them on his daily morning walks once said, "If you love anything enough, it will talk to you."

I invite you to be open to this by finding a plant in your own yard or other natural place close to where you live. Wander with an open heart, until you feel a strong pull from a certain plant. Don't choose it with your mind just because it's pretty. Instead, respond to whichever plant beckons you. You'll know the difference. Then sit quietly with your plant. Drawing it will help you appreciate its complexity and beauty and will still your mind. Tell it how you feel about it and just be with your plant. As you begin to have your own experiences, you'll learn to communicate in a way that is natural for you. It will take time, but it will happen, if you spend regular time with your plant and are attentive to whatever you feel or "hear." Whether it's the wisdom within you speaking or the plant speaking doesn't matter, because it may speak to you through your own wise self. What matters is the meaningfulness for you.

Finding the plant that beckons

Quaking Aspens in fall

What the Meadows Have Given Me

Page Meadows is named for John and Frances Page, who grazed their dairy cattle here from 1863 to 1880. I'm grateful that cattle no longer graze here, and that the meadows are preserved forever. Over many years, I have wandered through the meadows to find my favorite plants that bloom each year in the same special gardens. On some days, I just daydreamed in a sunny field of yellow buttercups. At other times I've found shelter from the heat of a warm August afternoon in a damp, shaded grove of Alpine Lilies. As the aspens turned golden in fall, I'd return for another kind of beauty. I've also cross-country skied through the meadows imagining all the millions of tiny seeds beneath the blanket of snow that will emerge again as spring warms the soil. These are the experiences that bring me back to the flowers again and again and are probably what draw you into Tahoe's backcountry and to other wild places. Page Meadows is a sacred place to drop our cares for a while and rest held in the peace and beauty of Nature.

#12 Sherwood Forest

Sherwood Forest garden

👢 👢 👢

One Way: 2.5 miles
Trail Begins/Ends: 7,100′/7,500′
Map: AM: Lake Tahoe Basin
Wildflower Season: June to September

Sherwood Forest is a magical place with vibrant wildflowers, expansive views of Lake Tahoe, and waterfalls that cascade into flower-lined creeks. The hike is in a huge, open bowl on the backside of the Alpine Meadows Ski Area with surprises all along the trail. There are Sunflower plants that create two different kinds of flowers in one flower, and a flower that is robbed by honeybees but pollinated by hummingbirds and bumblebees. This cross-country hike ends in a flower-filled meadow by a waterfall that cascades down a dark cliff to mist nearby nodding columbines. In the creek below the falls, Rock Fringe spreads its small leaves and pink, satiny blossoms over moist soil.

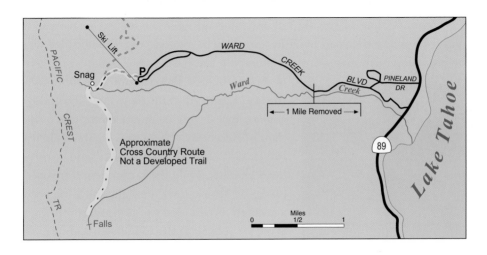

Featured Flowers

Arrow-leaved Balsamroot (*Balsamhoriza sagittata*)
Mountain Mule's Ears (*Wyethia mollis*)
Naked Broomrape (*Orobanche uniflora*)
Rock Fringe (*Epilobium obcordatum*)
Crimson Columbine (*Acquilegia formosa*)
Wavy-leaved Paintbrush (*Castilleja applegatei*)

Trailhead Directions: **From Tahoe City on Highway 89**, drive south 2 miles to the two, tall Pineland signs or **from South Lake Tahoe on Hwy 89** drive north 23.2 to the signs and onto Pineland Drive. Follow the yellow lines and as the road forks, take Twin Peaks Drive, which shortly becomes Ward Creek Blvd. Later the road is named Courchevel Road and then Gstaad. Parking for Sherwood Forest is along the road and is reached in about 4 miles from Highway 89. It is by Alpine Meadow's Sherwood Forest ski lift. The unsigned hike is user-created and mainly crosscountry. After parking, look southwest up to the ridgeline and to the highest patch of conifers. The Pacific Crest Trail is on top of the ridgeline. Our destination is a large, lush meadow well below the steep pitch of ridgeline and to the left of those trees.

Hike destination below ridgeline

The trail begins on the ski hill service road near the locked restroom. If you walk along the road in June and July in a good year, the hillsides will be blooming with many flowers including the yellow, daisy-shaped flowers

Balsamroot

Mule's Ears

Mule's Ears "ears"

Mule's Ears ray and disk flowers

of **Arrow-leaved Balsamroot** and **Mountain Mule's Ears**. At first they may look very similar, but if you compare them, you'll see their differences. The large, sparsely hairy leaves of Balsamroots are basal and arrow-head shaped, while the large, densely haired leaves of Mule's Ears are long and wide with a pointed or rounded tip. Balsamroot flowers grow singularly at the top of stems above the leaves, but Mule's Ears flowers grow along leafy stems, often tucked in the leaves. Knowing this, you'll never be confused again . . . at least by these plants! "Mule's Ears" refers to its young leaves that peek out of the soil in early spring resembling little, furry mule's ears. "Arrow-leaved Balsamroot" is for its arrowhead-shaped leaves, and "balsam" for its resiny taproot. Take a moment now to sit down by these two plants to become acquainted with their daisy-shaped flowers to learn something interesting about them.

Getting Acquainted with a Daisy

Everyone is familiar with a daisy, aren't they? Well . . . maybe not! Most people think a daisy is a flower with petals surrounding "things" in the center. But in looking closely, you'll find that it's actually a collection of many individual "disk flowers" in the center with one-petaled "ray flowers" surrounding them. See photo at left. After asking permission, gently remove one of its petals. Open the overlapping petal base to see the thread-like style attached to the tiny greenish ovary. The ovary houses an ovule or unfertilized "egg" that becomes a seed. Since a flower is the structure that houses reproductive parts, each daisy petal is actually a one-petaled flower with one female reproductive part, called a pistil. The ray flower is female, because it lacks the male stamens. Botanists call these "ray flowers," because they radiate outward, like rays of the sun.

Now look closely at the tiny greenish or yellow "nubbins" in the flower's center and the tiny yellow, 5-petaled flowers surrounding the nubbins. These are all tightly packed flowers either in bud (the green or yellow nubbins) or they are in bloom. Botanists refer to these central flowers as "disk flowers," because they grow in a disk-like circle. Unlike the pistil-only ray flowers, the disk flowers contain both stamens and pistils, so the pollen produced in the daisy flower form comes only from the central disk flowers.

The Daisy's Amazing Pollination Process

The reproductive parts in a daisy tell an interesting story. In comparing the thread-shaped styles of both the ray and disk flowers, notice that some are thread-like and others are 2–3 lobed at their tip. The lobed part of the thread-shaped style is the stigma or the part that receives pollen to fertilize the flowers. When ovules are mature and ready to be fertilized, the stigma opens to receive pollen from visiting insects.

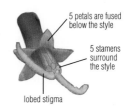

5 petals are fused below the style

5 stamens surround the style

lobed stigma

Disk flower with 2-lobed stigma   Ames Gilbert

To understand the process, you'll need to remove a disk flower and ray flower, after asking permission of the flower and thanking it. Then look closely at this "thread" in just the disk flower, with your hand lens. Do you see the vertical yellow or tan swelling on the thread-like style. This swelling is made up of 5 stamens, i.e. their vertical filaments and anthers, which surround the pistil to form an "anther tube." When the pollen is ripe, the anthers release their pollen grains into the center of the tube. Before the disk flower's ovules are mature, the style is way down inside the tube, but as the ovules start maturing, the style starts elongating.

As the style is elongating, its stigma remains tightly closed to prevent self-pollination in the tube. As the style elongates, it pushes the pollen grains ahead of it up the tube and out onto the tube's upper edge, where the pollen can be picked up by pollinators. After its own pollen is picked up by insects, the stigma opens into 2 or 3 lobes when it is ready to receive fresh pollen from another flower of the same species. If the stigma is not pollinated within a specified period of time, the style will actuallly bend down and curl around to self-pollinate from the few remaining bits of its own pollen. In doing so, it creates a clone of itself.

Leichtlin's Mariposa Lily

Rufous Hummingbird
seeks nectar from a drying
Horsemint

Nancy Gilbert

Western White Pine

Even without a hand lens, the lobed stigma is visible. Can you look at each flower and now tell the story of what is happening? Is the stigma tightly closed or is it lobed and ready to be pollinated? How did this little flower come up with such an intricate, amazing process? Maybe this is why botanists move so slowly . . . our slow wandering comes from a passion to go more deeply into the beauty and mystery of each flower and all of Nature. As Albert Einstein once said, "The most beautiful thing we can experience is the mysterious. It is the source of all art and science . . . He (or she) to whom the mysterious is a stranger, who can no longer pause to wonder and stand rapt in awe, is as good as dead."

The Road Becomes a Trail

Continue along the flowery lined road to where it turns right to head uphill. Instead, you'll head left onto the level, dirt trail until it dies out near a lovely waterfall on Ward Creek. You may see a Rufous Hummingbird, since our late local bird expert, Michael Jeneid, confirmed a new sighting of it and its nest here, though they don't normally nest at this elevation. The female leaves her territory to visit the male when she is ready to mate. After building a tiny, cup-shaped nest in trees or shrubs, she lays small, white eggs. The Rufous is about 3" long, yet can fly thousands of miles after wintering in Mexico to reach Alaska where they normally breed.

After the falls, head uphill on a short, gradual climb through a dry habitat to find Leichtlin's Mariposa Lily (*Calochortus leichtlinii*) blooming among rock slabs in June and July. It grows 4–12" tall with 3 greenish sepals and 3 white petals decorated with yellow nectar glands and a dark maroon spot. As you move higher, you'll arrive at a large, solitary Western White Pine (*Pinus monticola*) growing with regal dignity backdropped by Lake Tahoe.

In this dryish area, look for the orange, twining stems of the parasitic Dodder. Since it lacks chlorophyll, it lives by parasitizing other plants, and eventually it ungratefully strangles its host plant. In spring, the Dodder blooms with tiny, white flowers and then releases seeds that germinate to send rootlets into the ground.

As the stem grows, it searches for a plant to encircle. If it finds none, it soon withers and dies. If it finds the right host plant, it encircles the host and grasps it tightly with thread-like suckers. These suckers grow out of the stems of the Dodder and are called "haustorias," which is Latin for "drink." After its haustorias penetrate the tissues of the host plant, the Dodder's main roots begin to die and become useless within a day or two. Soon the orange stems begin encircling and climbing to the top of the host plant. After the Dodder is secure in its new environment, it again produces clusters of tiny, white, bell-shaped flowers, which after fertilization produce the seeds that begin the process anew. Dodders are perennials and able to live for many years on a host plant, but as they increase in size, they can eventually kill the plant, which causes their own demise.

Parasitic Dodder

A Creek Crossing by the Snag

Soon you'll arrive at an old, white snag. Head left there to cross over the creek, where you'll see pink Elephant's Head, orange Alpine Lilies, and red Crimson Columbines near pink Lewis' Monkeyflowers, which bloom on shrub-like plants up to 4' tall. If you sit quietly, a Sphinx Moth may appear and hover over the Monkeyflowers to sip their nectar.

Snag by the creek crossing

After crossing the creek, make your way uphill through a forest of fallen trees, ferns, and the white flowers of the False Solomon's Seal, until you see a clearing to the left through

Lewis' Monkeyflowers

Receptive stigma of Mallow

Naked Broomrape

the trees. At this point head out into the clearing, and you'll find a small meadow of White-veined Mallows (*Sidalcea glaucescens*). Can you find their lobed, receptive stigmas?

Continue uphill several hundred yards to a mossy, seep garden to find the 2″ tall plants of **Naked Broomrape**. Its lavender or yellow, glandular flowers bend forward to offer themselves to visiting insects and delighted botanists. broomrapes lack green leaves and so live as parasites, consuming nutrients from the roots of neighboring plants such as sedums and saxifrages. After climbing to a flat area just above the Broomrapes, veer to the left or south through an open, dry habitat of ground-carpeting Phlox, sedums, Wandering Daisies, and Sulphur Flowers. Continue through the open country and conifers without a trail, gradually heading uphill along the contour lines to reach the large meadow that is below the slope break and by the Crimson Columbine's waterfall.

Arriving at the Falls

In July through August, this part of the bowl usually explodes with color. Blue to lavender Large-leaf Lupines, pink Elephant's Heads, Giant Red Paintbrushes, and yellow arnicas all bloom together. As you wander among the flowers, take a moment to kneel down among the arnicas to check out their ray and disk flowers. After enjoying the view of Lake Tahoe, look near the creek for the vibrant pink 1″ wide flowers of **Rock Fringe** growing among

Rock Fringe

rocks and fallen logs. Rock Fringe is one of Tahoe's treasures with satiny blossoms and small, ground-carpeting leaves. The petals' tips have two rounded lobes, and its fresh white anthers surround the style, which bends out of the way until its pollen has been released. Then the style moves back to the center and opens its 4-lobed stigma ready to receive pollen from another Rock Fringe.

Higher up by the falls, **Crimson Columbines** bloom with unusual flowers. Take a few minutes to see if they are visited by a pollinator, but first notice that they have 5 vertical, dunce-caplike petals that are red and yellow. At the "cap's" top, there is a swelling with nectar. The flaring red structures, which seem like the petals, are actually sepals. You can see this when you look at the flowers in bud. Hummingbirds and bumblebees pollinate columbines and have no trouble reaching up the petal "caps" with their long, feathery-tipped "tongues" to sip the sweet nectar. Honeybees approach the flowers differently.

Crimson Columbine

They have a short proboscis ("tongue"), so they can't reach all the way up the cap for the nectar, but that's no problem. They just fly up to the top of the nectar-filled tip, grab hold, and bite a tiny hole in the side to effortlessly steal the flower's nectar without pollinating it.

On the rocky hillsides by the waterfall, you'll find the bright pink flowers of Mountain Pride, yellow Sulphur Flowers, yellow Mule's Ears, blue to lavender Spurred Lupines, and the red **Wavy-leaved Paintbrush**. Its bright red bracts hide its inconspicuous white to greenish, tubular

dune cap petals

sepals

Crimson Columbine

Mountain Pride

Sulphur Flowers by the upper waterfall

flower, which is pollinated by various hummingbirds. Like other paintbrushes, it is parasitic and so is often seen at the base of willows as it sucks up their nutrients and water. It also photosynthesizes with its green leaves. Looking down on its flowers gives a startling perspective.

The photography in these gardens can be spectacular in the late afternoon light, when the flowers glow with intense color. They are also especially beautiful after a storm when the air is still misty and the sky is overcast. Then the translucent light creates an intensity of color that shines from every angle. At such times, the flowers radiate a lively energy field that some believe is from the spirits who attend to Tahoe's lofty trees and wildflowers. Our world is full of magic, so who's to say that such spirits don't

Wavy-leaved Paintbrush by the falls

Looking down on the Paintbrush

Spirit of the forest

exist? If you come here some evening and sit quietly below the waterfall or nestle in the trees, the spirits might appear to express their joy for your presence. As you take the easy walk back to your car through the flowers and trees, perhaps under a full moon, be sure to express your gratitude for this vast, beautiful garden and for the spirits that inhabit Sherwood Forest.

#13 Hidden Meadow

Hidden Meadow
Geoff Griffin

One-way: 1.5 miles
Total gain: 380′
Map: AM: Lake Tahoe Basin
Wildflower Season: May through August

Large, peaceful Hidden Meadow blooms like a wild "bouquet." It is an easy hike for young children or for those who just want a leisurely walk among the flowers. A conifer forest is reached first with Snow Plants that bloom with shocking-red flowers. In open areas, a lush seep garden of wildflowers blooms with more bright colors. In the meadow, tiny green and white orchids, blue gentians, and other unusual flowers grow among the grasses. This very special hidden place is best experienced with a quiet mind, but if you bring a busy mind, the meadow will do its magic on you.

162

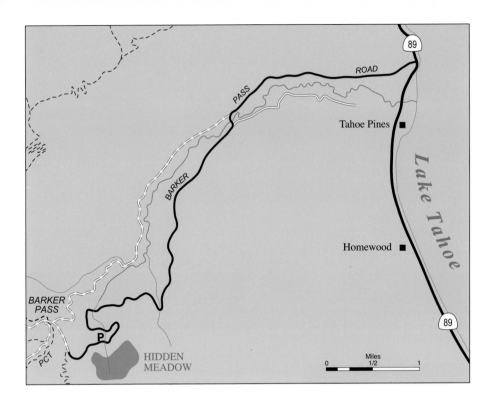

Featured Flowers

Mountain Larkspur (*Delphinium glaucum*)
Hooded Lady's Tresses (*Spiranthes romanzoffiana*)
Hiker's Gentain (*Gentianopsis simplex*)
Explorer's Gentian (*Gentiana calycosa*)
Western False-asphodel (*Triantha occidentalis*)
Grass-of-Parnassus (*Parnassia palustris*)

Trailhead Directions: **From Tahoe City** on Highway 89, drive 4.5 miles south to the Kaspian sign. **From South Lake Tahoe**, drive about 22 miles north to the sign. Turn onto blacktopped Barker Pass Road. After driving 2.3 miles, cross the bridge over the Middle Fork of Blackwood Creek and drive another 4.1 miles to a small turnout on the right. This parking area is just past a creek from the meadow that cascades down rocks by the road and then under the road. After parking, cross over the road and head back

Roadside creek cascades

Creekside garden

Mountain Larkspur and its flower

to the left side of the creek. Even though there is no sign or trail, Hidden Meadow is easily reached by keeping the creek on your right.

The hike begins on a short uphill climb through Red Firs and then levels out among yellow Heartleaf Arnicas and red Crimson Columbines, lit by shafts of golden light in the forest. Soon you'll reach a small meadow with flowers flowing down the hillside to the creek below. In June and July, the 5–6' tall **Mountain Larkspur** is found here with large palmately lobed leaves and tiny blue flowers that peek out from blue, petal-like sepals. In bud, the flowers look like tiny dolphins, if you have a good imagination. Its genus name "Delphinium" is Latin for "dolphin." The whole plant contains poisonous alkaloids, which if consumed in large amounts, can cause paralysis and death by asphyxiation. Alkaloids are naturally occurring substances produced by plants, and although they are toxic some plants with alkaloids are used medicinally. The alkaloids in quinine treat malaria, and those in morphine are used for their pain-killing, narcotic affect.

The tall Monkshood (*Aconitum columbianum*) grows here also on 4–5' tall stems with palmately lobed leaves. The flower's blue, petal-like sepals are shaped like a tiny monk's hood with reproductive parts that peer out from hood. The inside of the flower is perfectly shaped to accept bumblebees who are their main pollinators. Monkshoods are interesting, because some of their plants produce tiny bulbils in the axils of their leaves. Bulbils are green, vegetative buds that fall to the ground and root to produce clones of the parent plant. The whole plant is toxic, so some Native Americans used its poison to coat their arrowheads. You'll also see the Giant Red Paintbrush, Arrow-leaved Butterweed, Spurred Lupine, and White-veined Mallow.

Monkshood

Arriving in Hidden Meadow

After these hillside flowers, you'll wander through shaded woods past Snow Plants, Coralroot Orchids, and White-veined Wintergreens, until you begin to catch glimpses of Hidden Meadow. Upon entering the meadow, notice that the meadow winds its way to the left in an inviting, long expanse of lush grasses and flowers. Down in the grasses, you'll find "belly flowers," a term used by botanists for small flowers that are best viewed on one's belly. Pull out your hand lens and see what you might find. One tiny belly plant is the ¼" wide, pink to white flowered Graceful Phlox (*Microsteris gracilis*) each with its tiny blossom tucked down in the calyx. It grows 4–8" tall with lance-like, glandular leaves.

Monkshood flower

Graceful Phlox

Primrose Monkeyflower

Plantain Buttercup

Children enjoy peaceful moments too

In very boggy areas, look for the yellow Primrose Monkeyflower (*Mimulus primuloides*). It's a happy little flower that blooms with a solitary blossom on a delicate stem. Another yellow flower is the Plantain Buttercup (*Ranunculus alismifolius*), which blooms with shiny petals above narrow leaves that are up to 6″ long. Children love such small flowers, because they too are little and have no trouble getting down on their bellies to look at both the flowers and any small bugs that may be crawling over the mosses or through the grasses.

Children's Love of Nature

Children are born with a delightful, natural love of nature. Once, I was by my backyard pond with my grandchildren, Cooper and Aurora. My granddaughter and I were chatting away, when I noticed that Cooper, who was about 4 years old, had become very quiet and was squatting spellbound, looking up at tiny seeds drifting away from a tall willow. I went into my teacher mode and said, "Oh honey, did you know that those are the little seeds of the willow?" He didn't stop to look at me, thank goodness. He just continued intensely watching the seeds drift away, and said, "I know gramma . . . I just love 'em." He filled my heart with joy . . . I was struck by how important it is to pause in such precious moments and just be quietly present, without any teaching.

Unfortunately, we know that many of our children don't have such moments in nature and are losing this kind of connection by spending too much time indoors with computers, cell phones, and television. We all need such quiet time for our mental and emotional health. Outdoor play with other children, without adult supervision, is also a very important part of childhood growth. Chief Luther Standing

Bear, a Lakota Sioux (1868–1939) wrote, "The old Lakota was wise, he knew that man's heart away from Nature becomes hard; he knew that lack of respect for growing, living things soon led to lack of respect for humans too, so he kept his youth close to its softening influence." I'm glad that I now see more young families on the trail, who value these experiences and share them with their children.

Exploring the Meadow Flowers

As you wander by the creek, one of the most unusual flowers you may find blooming in the meadow will be the **Hooded Lady's Tresses**, a white flowered orchid with the complicated botanical name "*Spiranthes romanzoffiana.*" Its flowers are coiled somewhat like braided hair and so are named from Greek "*speira*" for "coil" and "*anthos*" for "flower." "Romanzoffiana" honors a Russian count and patron of science who lived in the early 1800s.

Hooded Lady's Tresses

Jim Fowler

Lady's Tresses is 6–12″ tall with grass-like leaves and has evolved an amazing way to distribute its pollen. Its pollen grains are clustered in a sticky mass, called a "pollinia," and are held on a protruding, sticky structure. When a bee flies to the flower, she touches the sticky pollinia, and it attaches to her and is separated from the flower. Once the pollinia has been released from the flower, the flower's style moves into the right position to receive pollen from another visiting bee. If a bee has a pollina attached to her forehead, she will touch the stigma on the tip of the style of that flower and pollinate it. After about 10 minutes, the pollinia structure falls off, and the bee flies to another flower and repeats the process. It's extraordinary that such a process could have evolved even once, and yet Nature is full of such surprises.

Bumblebee and pollinia

Nancy Gilbert

You'll also find two other orchids in the meadow by the creeks. The White-flowered Bog Orchid (*Platanthera dilatata* var. *leucostachys*) grows on stems from 8–30″ tall with numerous

Dragonfly on White-flowered Bog Orchid

Sparsely-flowered Bog Orchid

white, tiny orchid flowers. See pp. 100 and 181. Be sure to inhale its lovely fragrance. It is pollinated by the gossamer winged Four-Spotted Skimmer Dragonfly. The other Sparsely-flowered Bog Orchid (*Platanthera sparsiflora*) has green to yellowish flowers that are tiny, and it grows 18–24″ tall. The botanical name is odd, because though this orchid sometimes has few flowers, it also has been known to have 100 or more per stem. It is thought to be pollinated by moths. All three of these orchids usually bloom in July to August.

As you wander in the meadow in July and August, you'll find other special flowers in bloom. Of course, all flowers are special, but these two flowers are especially special! **Hikers' Gentian** grows on plants up to 8″ tall. Its purplish blue, tubular flowers have four slightly twisted, flaring petals that are fringed at the top. Check out the stigma; it looks like a tiny, yellow, ruffled flower as it sits in the middle of its yellow anthers.

Explorer's Gentian grows here too with large, showy, deep blue flowers on dense, leafy plants up to 18″ tall, which in this meadow are unusual, because their petals are marked with white blotches that I haven't seen on any other Explorer's Gentians.

Explorer's Gentian

Hiker's Gentian

Hiker's Gentian stigma and anthers

Explorer's Gentian, unusually spotted

The **Western False-asphodel** grows next to the creek on naked stems up to 18″ tall with white flowers that grow in clusters. Its leaves are basal, narrow, and parallel-veined. Its tiny, star-shaped flowers have similar sepals and petals with white, protruding filaments and yellow anthers. The fruit is bright red as it swells with maturing seeds.

Western False-asphodel in bloom   *False-asphodel in fruit*

The False-asphodel was in the Lily Family, but genetic studies have now placed it in the Tofieldiaceae Family as a solitary genus and species.

The lovely **Grass-of-Parnassus** grows in wet areas up to 18″ tall, with spoon-shaped leaves. Its 5-petaled, white flowers are veined in pale green, and the flowers are on solitary stems well above the leaves. Five stamens support yellow to orangish anthers, and its 4 staminodes (filaments without anthers) are 3-pronged and tipped with what looks like glistening drops of nectar. Botanists believe that this plant originally had 10 fertile stamens, but over time 5 of the stamens were replaced with these unusual, infertile staminodes, which were more attractive to pollinators. It is called "Grass" for its grass-like leaves. "Parnassus" refers to the flower's elegance and beauty, inspired by numerous mythological stories about Mount Parnassus and the God Apollo. It also honors the Greek Goddesses who were said to have inspired beauty and elegance in literature, poetry, and art. This is a lot to put on a little flower, but in its own way, it certainly is charming and worthy of being appreciated. The Fringed Grass-of-Parnassus (*Parnassia fimbriata*) is also found at Tahoe, but it differs with white fringe along the petal edges.

Grass-of-Parnassus

Grass-of-Parnassus, Fringed

Hairy Paintbrush

Nearby, the Hairy Paintbrush (*Castilleja pilosa*) grows among the grasses on stems 8–12" tall. What you'll notice first are its velvety soft, light pink bracts that are often edged in white. Its greenish yellow, tubular flowers are tucked down inside the bracts, but somehow pollinators find them. Like other paintbrushes, it parasitizes the roots of host plants to sustain itself with their nutrients and water.

Bistort (*Bistorta bistortoides*) is often abundant in Tahoe's meadows and grows up to 2' tall with lance-shaped leaves. You can find it by looking for round-to-oval clusters of small, white flowers. Its reproductive parts protrude beyond the petals and are topped by yellow anthers. The flowers are sweetly fragrant initially but later smell like "yummy" decaying meat to attract flies and other insects.

On a Rainy Day

If you visit the meadow on a rainy day, you'll discover something unusual. Most plants close their petals on an overcast day to protect their pollen from the damaging rain, but some flowers respond differently. The white Umbel Family flowers of Gray's Lovage (*Ligusticum grayi*) bend downward and seem to have been damaged by the rain. See next page. What has actually happened is that the cells in the stems, below the flowers, have changed their shape, causing the stems to go limp so that the rain runs down the outside of the petals like an umbrella to protect the flower's pollen. Lovage flowers with ripe pollen are the only ones that bend downward to protect their pollen. The flowers that have already released their pollen remain upright. Somehow a message travels to the cells in the stem that says, "Oops better protect me, it's going to rain!" Those that have already released their precious pollen have nothing to protect so a message is not sent

Bistort

to them. As soon as the sun comes out, the cells expand and the stems stiffen and rise upward. The flowers that seemed damaged a few hours before, now brightly present their vital parts to visiting insects and to the warmth of the sun's rays.

Diversity as Nature's Way

As you wander through the meadow, allow yourself to visually "float over the whole scene" and then focus on the details of all the incredible beauty and diversity surrounding you: the sizes, shapes, and textures of the leaves . . . feel them, smell them, and if they have hairs, use your lens to see how the hairs differ.

Compare the vibrant colors of the flowers and the markings they've evolved to attract insects. Various insects are attracted to different colors. Some, like the bees, see the yellow and blue band of color but not the red, while butterflies see red. White flowers attract moths and other insects that have ultraviolet vision and are attracted to the white flowers' complex patterns. Look too at the unabashed beauty and complexity of their reproductive parts. If you viewed their colorful pollen grains under a microscope, their intricate beauty would astound you with the amazing variety of their other-world shapes. Pollen grains are distrib-

Gray's Lovage plant & flower

uted locally, but others are so delicate they can travel a thousand miles on wind currents to alight on far away stigmas of the same species.

Leaving the Meadow

As you prepare to leave the meadow and return home, stop for a few minutes to think about the extraordinary gift of plants and their wildflowers. They express the life force with such gentle grace as they joyfully appear each spring to brighten the warming soils, after the bitter cold of winter. On windy days, they give form to the wind as they dance, celebrating their flowery aliveness with vibrant color and sweet fragrance. They bloom whether anyone is there to see them or not, and they require no weeding or other tending by humans. We wouldn't exist without the plants, and warm-blooded animals would not have evolved without the concentrated food provided by the plants and their flowers. Feeling gratitude for these natural, amazing beings will send us home with peaceful hearts and the sweet memory of a day spent quietly wandering in this hidden meadow.

#14 Barker Peak Trail

Mule's Ears & Lupine hillsides

One Way: 2.5 miles
Trail Begins/Ends: 7,710'/8,100'
Map: A.M: Lake Tahoe Basin
Wildflower Season: June through September

The Barker Peak Trail meanders along the flanks of Barker Peak through a large hillside of lavender lupines, pink mallows, and yellow Mule's Ears and Balsamroots. An optional cross-country jaunt leads to a steep scramble up to the rocky summit of Barker Peak. Towering volcanic extrusions bloom along the trail with bright red fuchsias and yellow rabbitbrush. After a gradual downhill trail through a conifer forest of pink primroses and yellow arnicas and past a small creek of rare, deep blue flowers, the trail reaches its grand finale, a glorious seep garden of wildflowers that cascades down a hillside into an inviting meadow below.

172

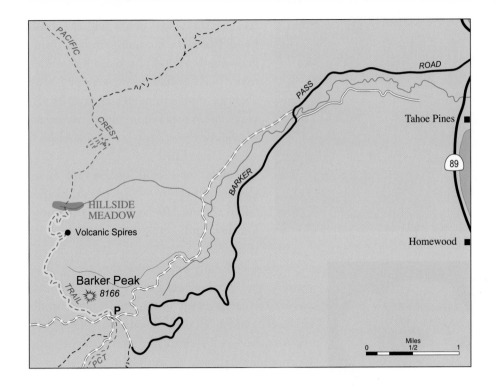

Feature Flowers

Ballhead Phacelia (*Phacelia hydrophylloides*)

Sierran Stickseed (*Hackelia nervosa*)

Spurred Lupine (*Lupinus argenteus* var. *heteranthus*)

White-veined Mallow (*Sidalcea glauscens*)

California Fuchsia (*Epilobium canum*)

Cusick's Speedwell (*Veronica cusickii*)

Trailhead Directions: **From Tahoe City** on Highway 89, drive 4.5 miles south or **from South Lake Tahoe** drive about 22 miles north to the Kaspian sign. Turn onto blacktopped Barker Pass Road. After driving 2.3 miles, cross a bridge over the Middle Fork of Blackwood Creek and then drive uphill past creek-fed gardens that bloom in July and August. After the road turns to dirt, it soon arrives at a road heading uphill to the right for the parking and trailhead, with restrooms and picnic tables for a total of 7.7 miles from Hwy 89.

The trail begins by the Pacific Crest Trail (PCT) & Tahoe Rim Trail sign and veers left through a mixed forest of Jeffrey Pines and Red Firs. At the

Ball-head Phacelia

Leichtlin's Mariposa Lily

base of the trees, you'll find the **Ball-head Phacelia** blooming in late June, growing 4–12″ tall. Its lavender to blue, fuzzy looking flowers grow in ball-head clusters, with extended stamens. Its velvety, soft leaves remind me of my favorite velvet dress that I wore to church when I was little.

Soon the trail enters an open, chaparral habitat of Sagebrush, Scarlet Gilias, Showy Penstemons, Wandering Daisies, and Leichtlin's Mariposa Lily (*Calochortus leichtlinii*), which grows 4–12″ tall with white flowers, golden centers, and dark nectar glands. John Muir discovered a mariposa lily in the California foothills in June of 1869, "Found a lovely white lily (*Calochortus albus*) . . . a most impressive plant, pure as snow crystal, one of the plant saints that all must love, and be made so much the purer by it, everytime it is seen. It puts the roughest mountaineer on his good behavior. With this plant the whole world would seem rich though none other existed."

In similar, dry areas look for the Wavy-leaved Paintbrush (*Castilleja applegatei*) that grows from 6–18″ tall

Paintbrush and Larkspur

Nuttall's Larkspur

with wavy edged leaves. It is often interspersed with the vivid colored Nuttall's Larkspur (*Delphinium nuttallianum*) that also grows from 6–18″ tall. Its purple to blue-purple sepals surround teensie flowers with white upper petals and blue-purple lower ones that peek out from the sepals.

The **Sierran Stickseed** grows nearby with stems up to 30″ tall. Its blue flowers have a central, white crown in the center, and the flower tube is longer than the calyx. Jessica's Stickseed (*Hackelia micrantha*) is often found nearby with smaller, blue flowers and flower tubes that are generally the same length as the calyx. Both flowers produce round fruit with tiny barbs, which cling to socks or to the fur of passing animals.

Sierran Stickseed

Jessica's Stickseed

Creative Seed Dispersals

Plants have devised many ingenious ways of dispersing their seeds, from stickseed barbs that cling to the fur of passing animals to the Dandelion's little "pappus parachutes," that distribute their seeds by wind. Pea Family flowers produce seed pods that twist so tightly as they mature, that the tension causes the pods to burst open and thrust their seeds far from the parent plants. Other plants, like cherries, thimbleberries, and blackberries, produce a seed or cluster of seeds that are surrounded by sweet, fleshy fruit to attract animals. Bats and other animals, after passing the seeds through their digestive tracts, eliminate them in their dung as little fertilizer packets to nourish the

Sierran Stickseed fruit

seeds after they germinate. Birds sometimes carry seeds across oceans, which is how some plants have migrated around the world.

Darwin discovered a wild tomato plant in the Galapagos Islands with a seed that won't germinate, until it passes through the digestive tract of one particular species of tortoise! The digestive juices break down the seed casing and allow germination to occur. Dispersal is not always the best option. Spotted Coralroot Orchids lack roots, so they drop their seeds at the base of their plants to guarantee that their young orchids will grow where soil fungi are present to sustain them.

Mule's Ears, and Heartfelt Song!

After passing through more groves of conifers, you'll cross a creek with Cow Parsnip (*Heracleum maximum*). Its white, umbel-flowered clusters can be up to 12″ wide, and they grow at the top of thick 5–7′ tall stems. Its leaves are up to 2′ wide and are palmately veined with serrated edges. The creek flows past alders and supports pink Lewis' Monkeyflowers, Giant Red Paintbrushes, and yellow Arrowleaf Butterweeds. At this point you'll be on an open hillside with distant mountain vistas and an uphill view of 8,166′ Barker Peak.

Cow Parsnip

In June to July, the hillside comes alive with the yellow, daisy-like flowers of Mountain Mule's Ears and Arrow-leaved Balsamroots. Standing among the flowers beneath a royal blue sky with white puffy clouds, you'll look out toward the distant, snow-capped peaks of Desolation Wilderness. You might feel that you've been swept away into a scene from *The Sound of Music*. You may be inspired to break out into song—let the moment capture you! Who cares if you're a little off tune? I'm sure the insect community will buzz with new delight as you add your voice to theirs.

Barker Peak Trail

As you walk along singing, you'll see the **Spurred Lupine**, which blooms with lavender to blue flowers among the Mule's Ears and Balsamroots. It grows up to 2½' tall and can be identified by the small swelling or spur on the back of the calyx and by the hairless tips of its wing petals. These plants often grow together, because they prefer volcanic soils, created from the ancient lava that once flowed through here. You'll also find a sprawling member of the Nightshade Family, the Dwarf Chamaesaracha (*Chamaesaracha nana*) with white flowers up to 1½" wide. "Chamae" is for "on the ground," and "Saracha" honors Isidore Saracha (1733–1803), a Benedictine monk and Spanish botanist who sent many rare plants to the royal gardens in Madrid. "Nana" is a botanical term for "small" or "dwarf."

Spurred Lupine

In June through July, look for a swath of pink below the trail from the flowers of the **White-veined Mallow**, who have something special to show you. Mallows are tiny versions of Hollyhock and Hibiscus flowers, with anthers that cluster tightly around the pistil. This is unusual, because most flowers have separate stamens with space between the anthers and an obvious pistil(s). Look closely . . . do you notice that some of the anthers just form a soft, white, fuzzy cluster, while others have a red "dot" in the center?

Spurred Lupine's keel

Dwarf Chamaesaracha

White-veined Mallow stigma

Other anther clusters have a tiny, red, lobed, thread-like structure. Do you know what is happening? The fluffy anthers mature first to release their fresh pollen. Then the style begins to elongate and peeks out of the cluster of anthers, like a red dot. When the ovules (unfertilized eggs) are ready to be fertilized, and the flowers have released their own pollen, the red dot, or stigma, opens into lobes to receive pollen from another mallow. This sequence of maturation is one of the most common devices that plants use to avoid self-pollination. Other flowers bend their styles to the side with a tightly closed stigma until the pollen has been released. Then they move back to the center and open like a tiny flower within the flower. Flowers aren't just "pretty, little, static things," they are magnificent little flower-people who change as they mature just as we do, and its fun to "read" these changes.

An Optional Climb to the Summit

After the mallows, you'll arrive at a three-way trail split. Take the trail to the right a few hundred feet up to the small saddle that looks out toward Lake Tahoe. From there, you can also look off to your left to see the volcanic extrusions on the ridgeline where you'll soon be hiking as the trail continues. To climb up Barker Peak, walk from the lake's overlook cross-country toward the east through the flowers and up to the rocky, south side of Barker Peak. It's a rock scramble, without a trail, to reach the bouldered summit. The view is gorgeous, and columbines bloom near the top, but the summit is precarious because of the steep drop-off. With good judgment, it's safe though it isn't a place for children.

Volcanic spires on trail

Continuing along the Trail

After enjoying the lake view or climb to the top of Barker Peak, return to the previous trail split and head to the right through the Red Fir grove until you arrive at smaller seep gardens of hillside flowers. The trail then heads back into more conifers and climbs up to reach the wind-swept ridgeline and the lichen-colored volcanic spires. Along the ridgeline, you'll find Lobb's Buckwheat (*Eriogonum lobbii*) lavishly spreading its leafless stems along the ground. A cluster of creamy flowers form a compact ball at the end of each stem. Its silvery, white leaves are velvety and grow as a basal rosette on the dry, sandy soil. I feel a fondness for this plant, because as the flowers age, they turn a rosy color, which is a sweet reminder that we too can become rosier with age.

Rondal Snodgrass

Author tucked in rocks near the summit

Lobb's Buckwheat

As you approach the spires in August or September, you'll find the **California Fuchsia** with striking, red flowers on low growing plants. Look at several of its flowers to compare their stigmas, and then think about how they differ from the stigmas of the mallows. The little nubbin at the end of the fuchsia's long style opens into a red, fuzzy, 4-lobed stigma after its anthers have released their pollen. Both open

California Fuchsia

lobed stigma

Receptive stigma of Fuchsia

Heartleaf Arnica

Rabbitbrush below spires

Cusick's Speedwell

stigmas on the mallows and fuchsias tells us that their ovules are ready and waiting to be fertilized. You'll also see the yellow flowers of Rabbitbrush (*Ericameria nauseosa*) with clusters of yellow disk flowers. Its linear leaves range from green to yellowish-green to white. The inner bark of this shrub was used by indigenous people to create a green dye, and the flowers were processed to create orange and yellow dyes.

By the PCT sign at the hairpin turn by the lava rocks, the trail heads down the west side of the ridgeline into a sunlit forest with yellow Heartleaf Arnicas (*Arnica cordifolia*). Its hairy leaves have an intense smell, and they are heart-shaped and opposite. Pink, evergreen Sierra Primroses (*Primula suffrutescens*) grow in the forest duff with bright pink flowers on naked stems 6–12″ tall. The trail soon breaks out into an open rocky hillside and then enters more trees before crossing a small seep garden where the small treasure, **Cusick's Speedwell**, blooms in July. It grows 4–6″ tall with 4-petaled, deep blue flowers marked with dark nectar lines. Two stamens with white anthers flare outward, and a bluish purple style extends away from the stamens.

Arriving at the Glorious Seep Gardens

After another short stretch of trees and 2.5 miles from the trailhead, you'll arrive at our final destination . . . a spectacular hillside meadow fed by melting snow that seeps down the hill to form creeks that flow across the trail down to the large, wet meadow below. Robust Lady Ferns grow 1–2' tall near Crimson Columbines, Cow Parsnips, Larkspurs, and Alpine Shooting Stars that bloom from June through July into August.

Lady Fern

The wet hillside also gives rise to the tiny, fragrant flowers of the White-flowered Bog Orchid (*Platanthera dilatata* var. *leucostachys*), which grow on 1–2' tall stems. Tahoe has at least six tiny orchids, which vary from ¼" to ⅜" wide. Orchids in South America tend to be larger and flashy with bizarre forms. The German botanist Breyneirs wrote, in the 17th century, "If nature ever showed her playfulness in the formation of plants, this is visible in the most striking way among orchids. . . . They take on the form of little birds, lizards, . . . of man and woman, of a melancholy toad, or a chattering monkey."

There is an orchid in South America that looks and smells like a female fly and is pollinated by the male fly in his attempt to mate with the female. Our White-flowered Bog Orchid smells like vanilla, but other orchids create a whole array of scents, choosing from at least 50 aromatic compounds. Out of these compounds, hundreds of variations are created with each species concocting its own scent. Sometimes the scents duplicate the fragrance of roses or other flowers. Some orchids even change their fragrances three times a day to attract the pollinators that are out at certain times. Other orchids create the smell of rotting meat to attract flies and other insects.

Later in the season, 3' tall Fireweed (*Chamerion angustifolium* ssp. *circumvagum*) blooms with pink, 4-petaled flowers. Notice that their white, extended styles have stigmas that open into 4 lobes. See p. 78.

Fireweed

Bee pollinating Explorer's Gentian

Western Aster

The Western Aster (*Symphyotrichum spathulatum*) blooms here in August with lavender flowers on stems up to 30″ tall. **Explorer's Gentian** also blooms in August with blue, tubular flowers on leafy, 18″ tall stems. Its luscious, dark blue buds remain closed for weeks before opening. They close their flowers at night or on stormy days to protect their pollen, saving their astonishing beauty only for sunny days.

As you stand or sit in the meadow, I'd like to leave you with the words of Chief Seattle (~1788–1866), which strike a deep chord in so many of us. In the mid 1880s he wrote a letter to the President in Washington expressing his anguish over the forced "sale" of his land. And though it is now thought that some one else wrote these words, they must have been in Seattle's heart. Below are excerpts, but ones I think you'll appreciate.

The President in Washington sends word that he wishes to buy our land.
But how can you buy or sell the sky? the land?
The idea is strange to us.
If we do not own the freshness of the air and the sparkle of the water,
how can you buy them?

So, if we sell you our land, love it as we have loved it.
Care for it as we have cared for it.
You must keep the land and air apart and sacred as a place
where one can go to taste the wind that is sweetened by meadow flowers.

Will you teach your children what we have taught our children?
That the earth is our mother?
We love this earth as a newborn loves its mother's heartbeat.

#15 Bayview Trail to Velma Lakes

Middle Velma Lake

👟👟👟 – 👟👟👟👟👟

One Way: 1 mile to Granite Lake
One Way: 4.5 miles to Middle Velma Lake
Trail Begins/Ends: 6,880'/7,960'
Map: AM: Lake Tahoe Basin or NG: Lake Tahoe Basin
Wildflower Season: Late June through August

The Bayview Trail offers stunning views of Lake Tahoe and Emerald Bay on the way to the Velma Lakes. Granite Lake is reached after a steep climb on switchbacks and is a pleasant destination for a short hike. The trail continues up a second, steep climb on more switchbacks until it finally crests a saddle with dramatic vistas and then heads downhill through a Red Fir forest. Pinedrops and the unusual, red-and-white-striped Sugar Sticks grow scattered on the florest floor. In sunny areas, huge boulders guard the trail like ancient sentries, until large, beautiful Middle Velma Lake is finally reached.

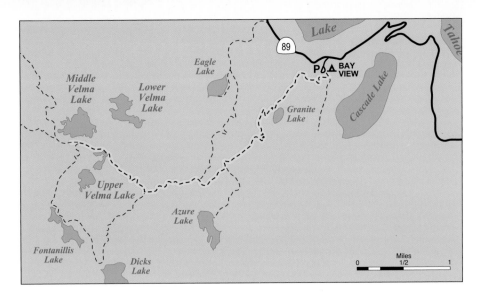

Featured Flowers

White-veined Wintergreen (*Pyrola picta*)
Bush Chinquapin (*Chrysolepis sempervirens*)
Huckleberry Oak (*Quercus vacccinifolia*)
Greenleaf Manzanita (*Arctostaphylos patula*)
Pinedrops (*Pterospora andromedea*)
Sugar Stick (*Allotropa virgata*)

Trailhead directions: **From Tahoe City**, take Highway 89 south about 19.5 miles to the Bayview Campground sign, which is about a mile south of Eagle Falls. **From the South Tahoe Y**, take Highway 89 north about 7.8 miles to the Bayview Campground sign. From there, follow the road through the campground to the day parking and Information board to pick up a permit to hike into Desolation Wilderness.

The trail begins at the fork just past the Information board and heads to the right into Desolation Wilderness on switchbacks beneath trees of White Fir and Jeffrey Pine. **White-veined Wintergreen**

White-veined Wintergreen

grows in the understory 4–12″ tall with creamy white flowers and showy styles. Their basal, evergreen leaves are marked with white veining, thus its name "picta," which is Latin for "decorated" or "painted."

Chinquapin's male flowers

At the beginning, you'll see the **Bush Chinquapin**, a chaparral shrub up to 5′ tall. "Chaparral" refers to fire-adapted shrubs that live in dry habitats throughout California and is derived from the Spanish "chaparro" for "evergreen oak." This is also the source of the name "chaps" for the leather leg protectors cowboys wear when riding through these dense, sometimes thorny shrubs.

Chinquapins can be identified by their dull green, leathery leaves and golden to rust-colored hairs underneath. "Chrysolepis" is Greek for "golden scale" for the hairs and "sempervirens" for "everliving" or "evergreen." Chinquapin's male flowers are creamy white with extended stamens topped by white anthers. The separate, inconspicuous, female flowers are usually directly below the males. Most plants produce both male and female reproductive parts in each flower, but the chinquapins are "monoecious," for "one house," because they produce separate male and female flowers

Chinquapin's spiny fruit

Red gall on Chinquapin's male flower

on the same plant. Other plants have separate male and female flowers on separate plants. After pollination, the fruit begins to grow and after two years, it matures into a ¾–1½″ spiny ball that encloses 1–3 brown nuts. The nuts were roasted and consumed by Native Americans and are also eaten by birds and rodents. You might also see bright red, large, cynipid wasp galls attached to the male flowers. A tiny female wasp starts the gall-forming process, after she deposits her eggs in the plant's tissue.

Huckleberry Oak covers the hillsides

Huckleberry Oak's male flowers

The Chaparral Community

The **Huckleberry Oak** is in the Oak Family with the chinquapins. It grows 2–4' tall with leaves up to 2" long that are green above and pale green below. Its tan, male flowers or catkins hang downward, and its tiny, creamy female flowers nestle in the leaf axils. Last year's brown acorns cling to the stems and in spring new, small, green acorns hide in the leaves. Look also for round tan galls, with brownish-red spots, attached to the branches. These galls are produced by another tiny Cynipid Wasp species, but the process is similar to the gall mentioned above. The female wasp pierces the stem tissue and inserts her eggs. At the same time, she injects chemicals that cause the gall to form aound the eggs for protection. As the larvae emerge from the eggs, they secrete chemicals that cause the gall to expand to both protect and feed them. The larvae live inside this thin skinned gall on central, spongy tissue that has spokes that suspend it inside the gall. The larvae secrete an enzyme, which converts the central, spongy tissue's starch into a sugar that the larva consumes. After it pupates into a wasp about the size of a fruit fly, it breaks through the gall's skin and flies away.

Huckleberry Oak gall and inside the gall

You'll also find two Buckthorn Family plants in the *Ceanothus* genus. Tobacco Brush (*Ceanothus velutinus*) grows 3–4' tall with clusters of white flowers and shiny leaves that emit a resiny fragrance. The similar looking, 2–4' tall Mountain Whitethorn (*Ceanothus cordulatus*) has white flowers, also in clusters, and white thorns on its white branches. These plants have identically-shaped flowers, as do other species in this genus. The flowers have tiny, spoon-shaped petals that extend outward from inward-curled, petal-like sepals.

A chaparral plant community is fire adapted and includes the Heath Family's **Greenleaf Manzanita**, which grows 3–5' tall with shiny reddish brown, exfoliating bark. Manzanitas are able to survive in dry habitats because of their long taproots. Their branches carry leathery, evergreen leaves and clusters of pink, urn-shaped, buzz-pollinated flowers. "Manzanita" is Spanish for little apple and refers to their small, apple-shaped fruits that turn from green to red. Native Americans throughout California made a refreshing drink from the fruit. They also dried the "little apples" and crushed them for their sugar to add to food. Pinemat Manzanita (*Arctostaphylos nevadensis*) carpets the ground up to 12" tall and creeps over rocks with white to pale pink flowers. Manzanita flowers are

Tobacco Brush

Mountain Whitethorn

Greenleaf Manzanita

edible and can be sprinkled on salads or other dishes for both flavor and color.

After a fire violently roars through a chaparral community, we lament the ugliness and apparent senseless destruction, but with the melting snows of spring, a miracle occurs. New life bursts forth from blackened stumps, as young sprouts grow out of root crowns of the chaparral plants. Melting snow and rains awaken new life in the seeds that have lain dormant under the shrubs for many years. The seeds are released from their dormancy when they are scarified by the fire and chemically stimulated by ash to germinate in the now fertile soil. Plant toxins, previously released into the soil over the years to inhibit competition from other plants, are destroyed by fire allowing new plants to grow and thrive again. Soon the chaparral community becomes green again and brightly colored with vibrant, new plants. Animals who survived the fire were protected in their underground homes.

Arriving at Granite Lake

Along the uphill climb, you'll be treated to gorgeous views of Lake Tahoe, Emerald Bay, and South Lake Tahoe. White Firs, shrubby chaparral, and dramatic boulders are strewn over the mountainsides. As the trail levels

out, the refreshing sound of Granite Creek can be heard, though the creek is hidden by the dense groves of 20′ tall Mountain Alders (*Alnus incana*). Notice their indented leaf veins and separate male and female catkins. The female catkins form tiny nutlets in brown, woody, cone-like structures, and the males hang downward. Alder roots house nitrogren-fixing bacteria that

Mountain Alder   *Alder's female catkin*   *Alder's male catkin*

convert nitrogen in the soil's air into a form that the alders can use. See Brewer's Lupines, p. 126. In the creekside's lovely gardens, there are also Bracken Ferns, Thimbleberries, Large-leaf Lupines, and Alpine Lilies.

Spreading Dogbane

In dry areas look for Spreading Dogbane (*Apocynum androsaemifolium*), which grows 6–12″ tall with small, pink, bell-shaped flowers and round to oval-shaped leaves. Honeybees are attracted to the flower's nectaries and sometimes can be seen grasping the flowers as they sip the nectar. Soon, you'll approach peaceful Granite Lake, which you'll see below the trail in the trees. You'll find you own easy way down the hillside to enjoy the lake, before continuing along the trail, unless you decide to spend the rest of your day right here.

Pinedrops and Sugar Sticks in the Forest Duff

After walking to the far end of the lake, the trail climbs up a series of steep switchbacks on a tough uphill for the next 0.75 mile, until it finally crests a saddle and levels out with great views into the backcountry. As the trail heads downward through a Red Fir forest, you'll find two very special flowers in the Heath Family: Pinedrops and Sugar Stick. Both plants lack green leaves so are unable to photosynthesize. Instead, they survive by parasitizing soil fungi in a mycoheterotrophic relationship. **Pinedrops** are tiny, urn-shaped, very sticky flowers that are pink, but soon become tan with age. On this trail, there are some stems that bend and curve as if dancing with delight. All parts of the plant have glandular hairs that contain special cells that release a sticky fluid to discourage ants and other inefficient, crawling pollinators. Pinedrops' microscopic seeds are released from the pods in the fall

Two-foot tall Dancing Pinedrops

Pinedrops' dried fruit

Sugar Stick flowers

by the thousands. Each seed has a little wing to catch the wind to distribute it far away from the parent plants. Its genus, *Pterospora*, is Greek for "winged seed."

If you're lucky, you'll find the elusive, startling, bright-red-and-white-striped **Sugar Stick** blooming in late June or early July. It grows 6–18″ tall scattered among the trees or peeking out from behind rotting, downed logs. If your mind is quiet and your heart is open, a Sugar Stick may allow you to find it. Don't strive to find it; just quietly ask if you may sit beside it to appreciate its beauty. This is how I found it in the expansive forest that surrounded the trail. It was on a day when there were only three plants in a small cluster in the whole area of the forest. It's aptly named and, in fresh bloom, it seems to sparkle with unusual beauty. Its small, white flowers face downward with five white petals that usually lack sepals. Its glossy, dark maroon to reddish anthers extend beyond the petals. A short style supports the red shiny, disk-like stigma that is surrounded by the red anthers.

Sugar Stick plant

Jeffrey Pine on Bayview Trail

Arriving at the Eagle Lake Junction

After a gradual descent past magnificent Jeffrey Pines growing out of the boulders, 2.7 miles from the trailhead, you'll arrive at a small saddle and a three-way junction with the Eagle Lake Trail. Head left on the sandy trail and in rocky areas, look for the 6–12″ tall, woody-stemmed subshrubs of Mountain Pride (*Penstemon newberryi*) with vivid pink flowers radiantly decorating rock outcrops. The tubular flowers with their woolly anthers invite insects to enter the flower's yellow-lined throat, with hairs that gather pollen from visiting insects. Its small, leathery leaves help it to reduce evaporation in dry habitats. Named after John Newberry (1822–1892), it honors his work as a physician and botanist who collected plants in California. He was also the first geologist to enter and describe the Grand Canyon.

The Sierra Onion (*Allium campanulatum*) blooms in the same area on naked stems 3–12″ tall with bright-pink, umbel-shaped flower clusters that are beautiful under a hand lens. Their 2–3 linear, basal leaves often dry up by the time the flower blooms. *Allium* is Latin for "garlic"; the leaves, flowers, and bulbs of onions were eaten by Native Americans. You'll also find Golden Aster, Pink Mountain Spiraea, Parish's Yampah, and Frosted Wild Buckwheat (*Eriogonum incanum*) with its clusters of small, separate male and female flowers on separate or dioecious plants. It grows 4–8″ tall, with leaves that have white, densely matted hairs. The similar dioecious plant, Marum-leaved Wild Buckwheat (*Eriogonum marifolium*), grows 4–16″ tall in similar habitats. Its pale yellow male flowers grow in small clusters; its bright yellow female flowers are larger and grow on spreading stems. Its leaves lack surface hairs but are white and densely matted beneath.

Velma Lakes' Trail junction

Mountain Pride

Sierra Onion

Frosted Wild Buckwheat

Bayview Trail to Velma Lakes   191

Arriving at Velma Lakes

In another 0.6 mile, you'll arrive at the Velma Lakes Trail junction. Head to the right over huge granite slabs past Pussy Paws, Whisker Brush, Lance-leaf Sedums, Nude Buckwheats, and Mariposa Lilies. In a dry year, the flower displays in these granitic, sunny areas are greatly reduced compared with the lush flowers in wet meadows or creeksides. Granitic soils don't retain moisture, like the humus-rich soils of wet meadows and creekside gardens, so wet environment flowers usually put on a fine display even in drought years.

Soon, you'll arrive at a pretty pond north of Upper Velma Lake. After walking along its north shore, you'll cross a creek and arrive at a junction. Now you can celebrate, because you have finally arrived at the Velma Lakes area after about 4 miles of a long, tiring hike. Here, lake lovers can choose from a banquet of lakes, each offering a different experience. One option is to take the 0.5-mile trail along the west side of smaller Upper Velma Lake, where you'll find good campsites and privacy.

For Middle Velma, continue on to shortly arrive at a junction with the Pacific Crest Trail for both the Fontanillis and Middle Velma Lakes. At this point those who want a longer hike can take the trail to the left for Fontanillis Lake and then return to Middle Velma, or take the 3-mile loop trail past Fontanillis and Dick's Lake and join the loop on the Bayview Trail to return

Pond above Upper Velma Lake

From shore of Middle Velma Lake

to the trailhead. Fontanillis, backdropped by Dick's Peak, is one of Tahoe's most beautiful lakes with many flowers around its shores and open views down to the Velma Lakes and Lake Tahoe.

To take the short jaunt to huge Middle Velma Lake, continue straight along the trail past a small meadow of yampahs and other wildflowers, and you'll soon reach the rocky hillside above the lake. From there, you'll look down on Middle Velma Lake and find your way down the sandy hillside to the lake's edge. Whether one lingers by the lake for the day, or for a night spent under the sparkling stars of Tahoe's night time sky, the lake's vast blue waters lap the shoreline with a rhythm that creates a deep sense of peace.

#16 Lyons Creek to Lyons Lake

Cascades on Lyons Creek

👢 – 👢 👢 👢 👢 👢

One Way: 4.8 miles to 8,400′ Lyons Lake
Other Option: Hike 0.5 mile to Lyons Creek
Trail Begins/Ends: 6,710′/8,400′
Topo Map: NG: Lake Tahoe Basin
Wildflower Season: May through August

The level, half-mile hike to where Lyons Creek is first accessed is great for a leisurely day of botanizing and wildflower photography and is an easy walk for youngsters. The creek flows over granite slabs into shallow pools, perfect for picnicking and wading on hot summer days. A curious, resident Marmot usually appears by the rocks at the creek's edge to check out new visitors. Wildflowers and bird life are abundant along the trail, and the final destination, 8,400′ Lyons Lake, is idyllic and scenic. After a reasonable uphill climb of approximately 4 miles beyond the first cascades, there is a steep, strenuous, uphill 0.4-mile climb to reach the lake.

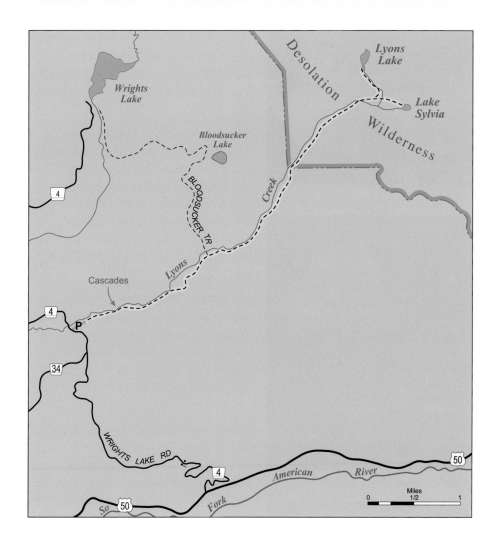

Featured Flowers

Fivespot (*Nemophila maculata*)
Naked Mariposa Lily (*Calochortus nudus*)
Sierra Mariposa Lily (*Calochortus minimus*)
Dusky Horkelia (*Horkelia fusca*)
Pretty Face (*Triteleia ixiodes*)
Musk Monkeyflower (*Mimulus moschatus*)

Trailhead Directions: **From South Lake Tahoe**, take Highway 50/89 and just after Meyers, take Hwy 50 to the west where it splits off from Hwy 89. Continue 16.4 miles to turn right onto Wright's Lake Road. **From Kyburz**, on Highway 50, head east about 3½ miles and turn left onto Wright's Lake

Fivespot

Naked Mariposa Lily

Sierra Mariposa Lily

Road. Continue for 4 miles and turn right at the Lyons Lake Trail sign and parking area. If you plan to day-hike past the creek cascades into Desolation Wilderness, you'll need a permit, which is available at the trailhead. For camping, you'll need to acquire a permit in advance. Call 877-444-6777 or the Ranger District at 530-647-5415.

The hike begins at the parking lot by a small meadow on an old road that soon becomes a trail. In June and July, depending on the snow, you'll find the flowers of **Fivespot**, which don't grow at Tahoe's higher elevations. It grows from 4–12" tall with white petals decorated with blue to purple spots. The dark nectar lines and tiny, pollen-like specks marking the petals entice pollinators, and its dark, curled anthers perch prominently on white filaments.

Two other treasures bloom more abundantly here and along the trail than anywhere else at Tahoe. The **Naked Mariposa Lily** grows 4–10" tall with lavender to whitish petals, purple to blue anthers, and purple lined nectaries. A white, 3-lobed ovary resides in the flower's center, topped with a pink, 3-lobed stigma. The white flowers of the **Sierra Mariposa Lily** bloom with white nectaries, and its anthers are blue, white, or purple but turn brown after pollination. A single, parallel-veined leaf stands above the flower like a sentry guarding a treasure. It usually grows in shady, grassy areas and under conifers. These two mariposa lilies hybridize freely, so identification can be difficult.

Over time, all species of *Calochortus* lilies have evolved special flower nectaries that secrete sugar solutions to attract bees and other pollinators. "Nectar" is from Latin for "the favored drink of the gods." There are thousands of bee species throughout the world that depend on nectar and pollen. Hive-creating bees convert nectar into honey and gather pollen for its protein, fats, and other nutrients, which they consume and save inside the hive during the winter to feed their larvae. These bees are clever

Bee gathering pollen

insects. They created the first air conditioner! During hot summer days, they gather water from a nearby source and deposit the water's droplets inside the hive. They wing-fan the droplets to evaporate the water, creating life saving cooling inside the hive. If temperatures in the hive rise too high, the colony will die. Bumblebees and other ground dwelling bees also gather and consume nectar and pollen.

Flowers in Sunny Openings

Dusky Horkelia grows about 12" tall near the beginning of the road, with pinnate, wedge-shaped, lobed leaflets and small flowers that cluster atop reddish, hairy stems. Pointed, hairy, pink-striped sepals appear between the 5 white, triangular petals that are two lobed and pink-lined at the base. Its creamy yellow anthers sit at the base of the petals, and a green ovary, with numerous stigmas, rises in the center. Horkelia honors Johann Horkel (1769–1846), a German physician, professor of medicine, and plant physiologist who discovered that plant embryos develop after fertilization.

Dusky Horkelia plant and flower

Slender Paintbrush

Pretty Face

Slender Paintbrush (*Castilleja tenuis*) is a small flowered annual that grows up to 8″ tall with white or yellow flowers nestled in sepals surrounded by dark-edged, green bracts. Its tubular flowers form 3 puffy sacs that meet in the center at a yellow spot by the upper, beak-shaped petal. **Pretty Face** grows nearby in drying soil with narrow, parallel veined leaves. Its yellow, brown-striped petals and sepals are identical. The stamens are unequal in length, and each filament has forked appendages at the tip to hold a blue anther. Tahoe's Mountain Triteleia (*Triteleia montana*) is similar, but its stamens are equal in length.

Torrey's Lupine

Dark-eyed Junco

You'll also find Torrey's Lupine (*Lupinus lepidus* var. *sellulus*) with blue to purplish flowers that are tightly clustered along 18″ tall, leafless stems. Its leaves are basal and palmate with five to eight leaflets. The upper banner petal is spotted white to yellow, and it turns reddish purple after pollination. Its pea pods are fuzzy and the peas are poisonous, since most lupine species concentrate toxic alkaloids in their peas for protection from nibbling animals. As you wander in the morning along the trail in the dappled light of the forest of Lodgepole Pines, Red Firs, and aspens, you'll hear many birds singing. Among them will likely

Torrey's Monkeyflower meadow

be the Mountain Chickadee, who sings Tahoe's sweet song of joy, and the White-breasted Nuthatch, an agile little songbird who scurries up and down trees foraging for insects, spiders or larvae. As it scampers straight down the tree, it stretches its little neck upward to look out at the world, undaunted by its precarious position as it clings to the bark. The Dark-eyed Junco is also easy to identify by its dark hooded head and the white flash of its tail as it flies swiftly through the air. The female Junco builds her nest and incubates her spotted eggs alone, although her mate helps feed their young.

The small, pink Torrey's Monkeyflower (*Mimulus torreyi*) carpets a large meadow next to the trail. Its three lower petals are striped with two yellow ridges edged in red. Near it in the same meadow, the non-native Sheep Sorrel (*Rumex acetosella*) grows about 18″ tall with tiny flowers that turn red in seed, and its arrowhead-shaped leaves have two small lobes at the base.

Sheep Sorrel

Flowers in Wet Habitats

As the trail passes wet meadows and crosses several small creeks, you'll find abundant Large-leaf Lupines, Coulter's Fleabane, Crimson Columbines, Corn Lilies, Arrow-leaf Butterweed, and the Giant Red Paint-brush (*Castilleja miniata*), which grows 1½–2½' tall. When you first look at the Paintbrush, you'll think you're seeing red "petals," but they are actually red bracts that brightly surround each greenish-yellow, tubular flower. Botanists believe that green bracts may have evolved over time into colorful bracts and then petals to more successfully attract pollinators.

Large-leaf Lupines

Giant Red Paintbrush

Did you find the flower? If you gently push the bracts aside, you'll find it inside the bracts. If the flower's tube and style are extended beyond the bracts, it is easy to see the flower, and it means the flower is ready to be fertilized. The three green nubbins on the lower lip midway down the flower are undeveloped petals. Paintbrushes photosynthesize in their green leaves and have roots that absorb water and nutrients, but paintbrushes are also partial root parasites. Their roots attach themselves to the roots of willows and other plants to absorb additional nutrients and water, so you'll often see this species tucked in under the willows.

In a lush side meadow, you'll also find the blue flowers of Leichtlin's Camas Lily (*Camassia leichtlinii*), which grows about 18" tall. It differs from the Quamash Camas Lily because its flowers are wider spaced on the stem and its petals drop off as the fruits ripen, whereas the Quamash petals twist around the ripening fruit. These two species can sometimes be hard to tell apart, because they hybridize. Be sure to wander into the meadow to see the other flowers.

Look low to the ground in shady, wet habitats for the **Musk Monkeyflower**. Its yellow flowers

Leichtlin's Camas Lily

have uniform petal lobes, unlike most monkeyflowers that have two obvious upper petals and three lower ones. Its leaves usually feel slimy. This cute little flower is scattered along the trail tucked in grasses or under other plants.

Using Your Hand Lens to Go Deeper

In small openings near the meadows and creeks, look for Tinker's Penny (*Hypericum anagalloides*), which spreads itself along the ground with creeping, rooting stems. Its stamens radiate outward with yellow anthers and surround the greenish ovary with a 3-lobed stigma. Now see if you can spot the tiniest flower of all along the trail, the Miniature Gilia (*Navarretia capillaris*). It's 3–4″ tall with tubular, ¼″ wide, white to pale blue flowers. It has flaring petals and blue anthers. All parts of the plant are very glandular hairy, except for the petals. Use your hand lens to see this. As you wander through these gardens, use your hand lens to look at other flowers too.

Flowers are amazing little beings that are very busy as they go about their daily business of living. If you slow down and actually take the time to look closely, in spite of perhaps wanting to continue along the trail, I think you'll discover a beauty that will enrich you in a new and unexpected way, and you'll certainly never look at flowers the same way again.

If you share the flowers with friends or children, it will be even more fun. Look at different flowers, identify their reproductive parts, and talk about how they differ. Look at the stamens and pistils . . . can you tell if the anthers are fresh or have dried up because they have released their

Musk Monkeyflower

Tinker's Penny

Miniature Gilia

Children are teachers too

pollen? How do the stigmas differ? Are some stigmas tightly closed, while others are open like a tiny flower? Do some stigmas glisten with a shiny substance? With time and your help, your children and friends will be able to tell a flower's story . . . like why its anthers release their pollen, why the style elongates, and why its stigma opens to receive pollen. Find your own words for this; it doesn't need to be technical! It's also empowering for children to realize that they too can be teachers by sharing with others what they've learned or discovered on their own. To approach flowers with this kind of interest is more fun than just walking by flowers with a glance, thinking you know them because you can name them.

Arriving at the Creek's Cascades

The trail passes lots of gorgeous flowers before it arrives at the first cascades on Lyons Creek, where you can relax before continuing on. You may even

Creek Dogwood

decide to spend the rest of the day here, if you are with young children. The shallow water and pools in the creek are safe for children, if you keep an eye on them. The 8' tall, white flowered shrubs of Creek Dogwood (*Cornus sericea*) line the creek, blooming with white flower clusters. In fall its leaves turn pink to yellow and orangish. The shrubs of California Mountain Ash (*Sorbus californica*) bend

Mountain Ash by the cascades

Mountain Ash in fall

over the creek with clusters of white flowers and serrated, pinnate leaves. Its leaves turn yellow to pinkish in the fall and its stems hold bright red berries.

In the rocks by the creek, you'll probably see the resident Marmot. It belongs to the Squirrel Family and is a brown, furry rodent with a yellow or orangish belly and a large bushy tail. Marmots generally live in groups and are more often found above the tree line in elevations up to

Marmot nibbling grasses

12,000'. They live in burrows carved under large rocks or beneath large tree roots that can't be penetrated by predators. They prefer meadows or other grassy areas, where they can nibble on grasses and other green vegetation. If they feel threatened, they warn other Marmots with a high-pitched whistle. In fall, they prepare for an 8-month winter hibernation by eating large amounts of greens, flowers, and seeds to build up as much fat as possible. Three to eight young are born in spring in their protected burrows. Mothers nurse their young for about 3 weeks, until the youngsters can forage on their own.

Continuing to the Lake

After leaving the creek, you'll soon begin climbing uphill on a rocky trail in open, dry habitats and through shaded groves of conifers. In dry areas, look for shrubby Pinemat Manzanitas (*Arctostaphylos nevadensis*) carpeting the ground and even boulders with their mahogany colored stems, leathery leaves, and small, white, urn-shaped flowers. You may see red swellings on the edges of the leaves. Though some people mistake these swellings for fruit, leaves don't produce fruit! The swellings are galls created by mother aphids.

Aphid galls on Pinemat Manzanita

One-sided Wintergreen

Look in the shade under conifers for the One-sided Wintergreen (*Orthilia secunda*). It's also called "Sidebells" for the way its white to greenish, urn-shaped flowers grow along the nodding stems. It's usually found right at the base of conifers in the forest duff.

You'll pass larger, dramatic cascades whenever the trail is close to the creek. You'll also reach a sign at a junction, with the unappealing name, "Bloodsucker Lake." I can't imagine that anyone visits this lake! After crossing into Desolation Wilderness, you'll see a larger group of rock slabs with cascades flowing into deeper granite pools. As the open, rocky trail climbs higher, you'll have views of Pyramid Peak and reach another set of pools, before you cross Lyons Creek and head up to the lake.

In June, after a winter of abundant snow or rain, the water in Lyons Creek may be 12″ or deeper, so plan accordingly. If you are here in June, and crossing the creek feels too challenging, enjoy the flowers on the first few miles of the trail when the lower elevation plants are in full bloom. Return later in the season to hike to spectacular Lyons Lake for the later blooming, high elevation flowers. In late June to early July, you'll see early bloomers by the lake, and in a drought year, the creeks are lower and the flowers bloom earlier.

If you decide to continue on to the lake, after about 600′ past the creek crossing, you'll see a post marking the steep, rocky, uphill trail to Lyons Lake.

Geoff Griffin

Bog Laurels by the pond

As you climb, you'll have beautiful views of Pyramid Peak and the surrounding mountains, as the creek cascades down the slope on your right. When the climb comes to an end, it levels out by Mountain Hemlocks and a shallow pond, dammed near the trees by rocks. There, in late June, you may find buttercups along with Marsh Marigolds, Mountain Heathers, Cassiopes, and Bog Laurels.

Lyons Lake

Continue along the edge of the pond to the second, small, rock dam on Lyon's Lake to walk along it to the lake. There are a few scattered campsites and since this is such a pristine habitat, make this a minimalist camping experience to preserve its idyllic setting. Open fires are not allowed. Be sure to put your campsite back to normal before you leave, and of course don't leave any trash . . . of course, a flower person wouldn't do that!

Bog Laurel

It is even best to take a day hike here to minimize your impact but for that, you'll need an early morning start. The forest service also recommends camping 100′ from the lake. Let's keep this beautiful lake idyllic and pristine so at least seven generations or more can enjoy it for many years to come!

#17 Big Meadow to Dardanelles Lake

Big Meadow

🥾🥾🥾🥾

One Way: 4 miles
Trail Begins/Ends: 7,260'/7,760'
Map: AM: Lake Tahoe Basin or NG: Lake Tahoe Basin
Wildflower Season: June through August

The trail to Dardanelles Lake climbs uphill through a dense forest and crosses a flowery creek to enter impressive Big Meadow with wildflowers blooming in June to July. Beyond the meadow, shaded gardens bloom with Alpine Lilies, Large-leaf Lupines, and Thimbleberries, and in one area along the trail, bright red Snow Plants rise out of the forest duff in a startling display. The Washoe came to Big Meadow every summer and fall to enjoy its beauty and to fish, hunt, and gather plants. We'll imagine a day from their past on this hike. Several more flower-lined creeks are crossed before peaceful Dardanelles Lake comes into view.

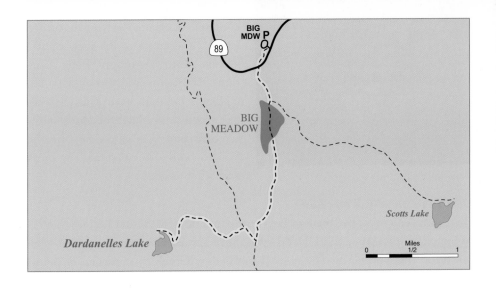

Featured Flowers

Hairy Arnica (*Arnica mollis*)
Tuber Starwort (*Pseudostellaria jamesiana*)
Snow Plant (*Sarcodes sanguinea*)
American Speedwell (*Veronica americana*)
Mountain Sagebrush (*Artemisia tridentata*)
Quamash Camas Lily (*Camassia quamash*)

Trailhead Directions: **From South Lake Tahoe**, south of Meyers where Highways 50 and 89 intersect, take Highway 89 to the left and drive 5.1 miles. Turn left at the Tahoe Rim Trail (TRT) sign and head down into the large parking area by the bathrooms and excellent informational boards that tell how the Washoes once lived.

The trail begins by the TRT sign in the lower parking area. It passes through a forest and crosses Highway 89 and heads uphill on a boulder-lined trail with shrubs of Whitethorn, Creeping Snowberry, and Wax Currant (*Ribes cereum*). This currant grows 5–8′ tall with clusters of pink, tubular, bell-shaped flowers that are followed by red, edi-

Wax Currant

Mountain Pink Currant

ble fruit. "Cereum" is from Latin for "waxy" and refers to its waxy-coated leaves. The Mountain Pink Currant (*Ribes nevadense*) grows 3–6' tall in damp habitats with pink flowers and clusters of bluish black, glandular fruit that was eaten raw by the Washoe and also consumed by birds and other animals.

The Junction with Scotts Lake

In about 0.75 mile, the trail arrives at the junction for Scotts Lake, which is worth a visit another time. Head straight past this junction, and you'll soon arrive at the wooden bridge over Big Meadow Creek by a garden of paintbrush, butterweed, Monkshood, and the Large-leaf Lupine (*Lupinus polyphyllus*), which grows 3–4' tall with blue purple flowers and palmately lobed leaves. Ranger's Buttons (*Sphenosciadium capitellatum*) grows in the same garden. As is typical in the Umbel Family, its flower stems radiate outward like the spokes of an umbrella. It grows 4–5' tall with white flower clusters that form dense, round balls, leading to its playful common name.

One half-mile-long Big Meadow opens up just past this garden. When I first walked into the meadow, I was thrilled by its size and by the flowers and grasses waving in the breezes under the open sky. I also thought of the Washoe people who spent time here for thousands of years fishing for Cutthroat Trout in the creeks, hunting near the meadow, and gathering plants for food and medicine. **Hairy Arnica** blooms in the meadow with hairy,

Large-leaf Lupines *Ranger's Buttons*   *Hairy Arnica*

fragrant leaves that grow in three to five pairs along the stem. Native Americans used their fresh leaves externally to heal bruises, sprains, and sore muscles. Other flowers in the meadow are discussed on other hikes, so check the "Flowers by Color" section to identify them.

Glorious wet garden

Beyond the Meadow

After leaving the meadow, the trail passes wet areas of aspens and Thimbleberries and then begins climbing uphill through a forest of Coralroot Orchids, Snowberries, Spurred Lupines, and Valerians. As the trail climbs up wooden steps, it tops out and then passes through a small, glorious wet garden of Corn Lilies, Large-leaf Lupines, Brewer's Angelicas, Arrowleaf Butterweeds, and Giant Red Paintbrushes. Look also for Coulter's Fleabane (*Erigeron coulteri*), which grows up to 2' tall with white daisy flowers.

Coulter's Fleabane

After the trail arrives at a saddle, it descends on switchbacks through a forest where the **Tuber Starwort** grows 4–18" tall with small, white flowers with five petals that are 2-lobed. Its anthers are bright red but fade to brown after releasing their pollen. "Tuber" is for its roots, which resemble small, brown skinned tubers or potatoes.

You'll soon arrive at a junction with the Meiss Meadow Trail, at 2.2 miles from the trailhead. Take the Lake Valley trail to the right for 0.2 mile, and at the next fork, take the trail to the left that heads west to Dardanelles Lake. As the trail descends, it passes a fabulous display of fleshy, bright red **Snow**

Tuber Starwort

Snow Plants along the trail

Plants that in 2015 numbered over 50 plants in this one small area. They grow under Red Firs, 6–12″ tall with nodding, bell-shaped flowers and red bracts. Snow Plants lack green leaves, so they are unable to photosynthesize. Instead they live through a myco-heterotrophic relationship with the False Truffle, a soil fungus that commonly lives in the soil by conifers. The fungi colonize the roots of conifers in a symbiotic relationship, increasing the conifers ability to absorb nutrients and water from the soil. The conifers produce carbohydrates through photosynthesis in their needle-like leaves, which the fungus absorbs as it colonizes the roots. The Snow Plant enters into this by being dependent upon the soil fungi for nutrients and water, which allows the Snow Plant to live in the shaded, forest duff where sunlight is lacking for photosynthesis. Such cooperative relationships are amazing, yet common throughout the plant world.

John Fremont was one of the first explorers to collect the Snow Plant, which he found in 1853 in North Tahoe along the Yuba River. When John Muir found it in Yosemite, he described it as a ". . . singularly cold and unsympathetic plant. Everybody admires it as a wonderful curiosity, but nobody loves it as lilies, violets, roses, and daisies are loved. Without fragrance, it stands beneath the pines and firs lonely and silent, as if unacquainted with any other plant in the world; never moving in the wildest storms; rigid as if lifeless, though covered with beautiful rosy flowers."

Nancy Gilbert

Male Western Tanager

Western Tanagers can be found here as they fly through the trees. The male is bright red and yellow with black and white marked wings; the female is yellowish with similar wing markings. These brightly colored birds fly up from Costa Rica, Mexico or sometimes from southern California to breed in Tahoe. They live in forests and at the edges of meadows and they catch insects in flight or among the needles of the conifers. They also consume berries and other fruit. The female builds a cup-shaped nest, high up on the branches of pines and firs out of pine needles and twigs, and she lines it with mosses. The male sings during nesting, and although only the female builds the nest and incubates the eggs, both parents feed the young until they fledge.

Finding the Trail to Dardanelles Lake

At 2.8 miles from the trailhead, you'll take the unsigned trail next to a pile of rocks by a large Western White Pine. After two creek crossings, the trail crosses a third creek on flat stones by monkeyflowers, columbines, Mountain Bluebells, and the **American Speedwell**, which grows up to 12″ tall with blue flowers marked with reddish purple. Two stamens and a style extend from the flower, and its opposite leaves grow at the nodes on its reddish-brown stems.

American Speedwell

After the creek, the trail takes a short, 0.3-mile climb uphill through Mountain Pride, Prickly Phlox, Creambush, and past large boulders and granitic slabs until it arrives at the shoreline of Dardanelles Lake. This large, inviting lake is at an elevation of 7,760′ with a granitic mountain at its edge. Its sparkling waters can be viewed from scenic campsites along a shoreline that meanders around to the right to a flat peninsula. Good campsites by the lake and the open sky make an overnight stay here under the stars a magical adventure.

How the Washoe May Have Lived

How exhilarating it must have been to spend their days outdoors among such lakes and wild gardens. They didn't need to pick bouquets of flowers to brighten their homes; their home *was* the outdoors, which was covered

Dardenelles Lake

Seep-spring Monkeyflowers

with gorgeous, living bouquets . . . so let's go back in time to imagine a day in the life of the Washoes.

It's a warm day in summer, and you are a young Washoe woman gathering tender leaves of monkeyflowers and various mustard greens for a salad as you enjoy the sweet taste of the thimbleberries and tiny, sweet strawberries. Later in the season, you'll gather currants, serviceberries, and rose hips along with the swollen bulbs and

Thimbleberry fruit

Wax Currant fruit

Mountain Pink Currant fruit

Rose hip

small seeds of onions and *Calochortus* lilies. The men have gone fishing or to hunt for rabbits and other game that will be roasted or added to stews.

As you hike the trail, mosquitoes attack, so you gather leaves of Mountain Pennyroyal to rub on your body. This helps to repel the mosquitoes. You also gather its leaves and white to lavender flowers to later brew into a mint tea, which you'll enjoy this evening as the sun drops down behind the trees. After the manzanita berries ripen in the fall, you'll gather them to make a refreshing, sweetened cider but earlier in spring, you'll enjoy the sweetness of their fresh flowers.

Mountain Pennyroyal

The warm summer breezes carry the aromatic fragrance from the leaves of **Mountain Sagebrush**, which reminds you of the special times these plants are used in sacred ceremonies to purify body and soul. You gather the leaves to use in a shampoo made with water infused with *Ceanothus* blossoms. You also gather and crush last year's dried leaves that have fallen to the ground to make an antiseptic diaper powder for your baby brother.

Pinemat Manzanita fruit

With your fire-hardened stick, you'll dig up sweet Yampah bulbs and eat a few raw, before taking the rest home to be roasted over hot coals. In late summer, you'll join other women in the meadow to gather the sweet bulbs of the **Quamash Camas Lily**, digging them with fire-hardened sticks made from the Mountain Mahogany or manzanitas, while the men collect wood and green alder branches to place in an earthen oven. As you gather the bulbs, you'll scatter the small ones to encourage more plants to grow throughout the meadow, so the supply of bulbs will never be depleted.

Sagebrush leaves

Quamash Camas Lilies

After washing the bulbs in the nearby creek, you'll take them to the cooking area where the men have dug large earthen pits to hold the branches that have been burning to form hot coals. Green alder branches will then be placed in the pits above the hot coals with several layers of bulbs, ashes, and more hot coals, which will finally be covered with smaller branches, leaves, and grasses to bake for over a day. After removing the bulbs, while they are still warm, you help strip off their black fiber. As they cool, you'll sing and visit as you all press them into sweet cakes with the fragrant aroma of vanilla and the consistency of maple sugar. The cakes will be eaten warm and also stored for winter eating.

The Work of the Men

As you wander through the woods, looking for rose hips for tea, your brother appears. He has been out gathering material for the tools and weapons he has been making this summer. After searching out the elder-

Willow fluff

berries, cottonwoods, willows, and cedars, he chooses the best, straight branches and carves them into fire drills or flattens them to use as dill bases. You've often seen him and the older men vigorously rotate the drill between their palms or on a "bow string," until the friction magically creates a tiny burning coal. With the right timing and gentle blowing, it ignites the tinder that sits at the base of the drill. You have often helped gather the tinder from the dried and shredded inner bark of cottonwoods and the fluffy seeds of willows, fireweeds, and goldenrods.

Your brother is also gathering pine branches to make a new bow. He'll string his bow with deer sinew or the fibers he has prepared from milkweed. Small branches from the wild rose or willow shoots will be used to make arrow shafts that he will connect to carved obsidian or flint. It will be many years before he is skilled enough with his bow to hunt large game. Because your people's bows are short with a limited range, he must closely approach game with highly skilled techniques. In late fall you and your people will head down to lower elevations to spend the winter in a warmer habitat on the east side of the mountains.

The Fine Art of Washoe Basketry

As you arrive at a creek, you drink from its cool, sweet waters by willows growing thickly along the banks in summer and fall. Earlier this spring you and your teenage friends, who had arrived at Tahoe before the younger children, mothers, and elders, gathered the new spring shoots from willows. You had watched the women cut some of them back in fall to encourage long shoots so they would grow without side branches for the baskets. For years you have been working with your grandmother to learn how to make beautiful baskets. This summer she will help you make a very special one of your own design from red dogwood shoots and the bracken fern's black roots. These baskets are important for many uses from gathering and carrying to the storing and cooking of food. You remember as a child being

Willows in fall

Bracken Fern

amazed at how your mother and grandmother cooked acorn mush or roasted seeds in willow baskets with hot rocks without burning the baskets.

As the years pass, another Washoe woman, Dat-so-la-le, is born. She weaves baskets on the shores of Lake Tahoe at the turn of the century and with the help of a trader, she sells her baskets and becomes highly acclaimed for their masterful complexity and beauty. Her baskets offer both art and function in its highest form, and many years later they become valued at thousands of dollars each, though Dat-so-la-le earned little herself. Dat-so-la-le died in 1925, at the age of ninety-six. Knowing the Washoe history at Tahoe will inform and deepen your Tahoe experience and appreciation for them. The land at the Taylor Creek Visitor Center near South Lake Tahoe was a summer gathering and living place for the Washoe for thousands of years. The Center offers the lovely, level rainbow trail by the creek and includes a fish profile chamber. In the Information Center there is a beautifully designed, sensitive exhibit by the Washoe that honors their ancestors with deeply moving stories of their history and present life.

#18 Frog Lake to Winnemucca Lake

Winnemucca Lake

👟👟 – 👟👟👟

One Way: 2 miles
Trail Begins/Ends: 8,574'/9,500'
Map: AM: Lake Tahoe Basin
Wildflower Season: June through August

Winnemucca Lake is reached after smaller Frog Lake, which lies nestled in a grassy meadow with blue purple irises that bloom with regal grace. The short trail to Frog Lake is fun for young children, and the trail from this lake to Winnemucca Lake blooms with intense flower color usually in July. Plants that resemble tiny, pink Elephant's Heads bloom in seep gardens, and the unusual flowers of Sierra Claytonia and delicate Brook Saxifrage grow alongside creeks near bright pink Sierra Primroses. Tall Monument Plants put on a grand show with flowers that bloom along stems that tower over all other flowers on the open, sunny hillsides.

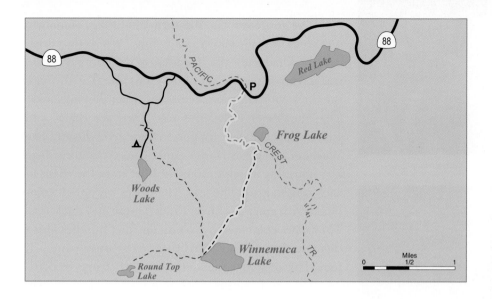

Featured Flowers
Western Blue Flag (*Iris missouriensis*)
Elephant's Head (*Pedicularis groenlandica*)
Little Elephant's Head (*Pedicularis attollens*)
Sierra Claytonia (*Claytonia nevadensis*)
Brook Saxifrage (*Micranthes odontoloma*)
Monument Plant (*Frasera speciosa*)

Trailhead Directions: **Take Highway 88** to 8,574' Carson Pass for trailhead parking by the Visitor's Center, where you'll be helped with updated flower information, books, and maps by friendly volunteers of the El Dorado National Forest Interpretive Association (ENFIA) (209-258-8606). A wilderness permit is required even for a day hike and can be picked up at the Center. There is a fee to park. Avoid weekends if possible.

The trail begins by the Information Center and heads uphill under Lodgepole and Jeffrey Pines and past pink Mountain Pride and Azure Penstemon. Within a half mile, the trail reaches smaller Frog Lake, before it continues on to wind swept Winnemucca Lake. In damp areas near Frog Lake, look for the California Hesperochiron (*Hesperochiron californicus*), which grows 1–4" tall with basal, hairy leaves and white to pink tinged flowers.

California Hesperochiron

Western Blue Flag

Wavy-leaved Paintbrush and Nuttall's Larkspur

Blue Flax

The gorgeous iris, **Western Blue Flag**, blooms in wet areas near the lake in early July. "Iris" is the classical Greek name for the "Goddess of the Rainbow" who was a winged messenger of the Gods that flew through the skies with a glorious rainbow for her flowing cloak. The Shoshones called this iris "Daw see doya" and gathered its rhizomes to poison their arrowheads. The Washoes and other Native Americans created cordage by separating a single strand of fiber from the edges of each tough, grass-like leaf. The fibers were then combined with more iris fibers to add length and thickness. They were combined by rolling the fiber bundles along their thighs, which caused them to be intertwined. It took days or weeks to months to made strings or cordage for carrying-bags, nets or ropes. Iris leaves were also woven together to make baby diapers, which were filled with cattail fluff.

In dry habitats near the lake, look for the 6–18" tall Wavy-leaved Paintbrush (*Castilleja applegatei*). It has wavy-edged leaves, and its yellowish, tubular flowers are surrounded with red bracts. Also look for the blue to lavender flowers of Nuttall's Larkspur (*Delphinium nuttallianum*), which grow up to 18" tall with blue, petal-like sepals that surround its tiny flower. The vibrant flowers of Blue Flax (*Linum lewisii*) also bloom in dry habitats on 1–3' tall stems. They bloom for one day and then drop their petals later in the day. The following morning new flowers bloom, decorating the plant with a lovely shade of blue. Native Americans made strings from the stems and cording for fish nets.

Rosy Pussytoes (*Antennaria rosea*) supports flowers that vary in color from white to pink on naked stems

Rosy Pussytoes

above small, basal, white hairy leaves. Its papery disk flowers grow on separate plants that are either female or male. Most of the plants will be females that clone themselves by runners and carpet the ground.

Along the lake, the five-needled Whitebark Pine (*Pinus albicaulis*) grows with red male cones and purplish female cones. They can be viewed up close, because the harsh conditions at this high elevation have pruned them into horizontal forms. At lower elevations, they often grow to a height of 70' making examination of the cones rather difficult, unless you are very tall! The fertilized cones grow erect the first year but by the next summer, they mature and become horizontal. The seeds are held tightly in closed cones, until they are extracted by birds or animals. See p. 242. The downward swooping branches and the buildup of needles form protective coverings and comfortable beds for animals and humans, as John Muir experienced, "During stormy nights, I have often camped snugly beneath the interlacing arches of this little pine. The needles, which have accumulated for centuries, make fine beds, a fact well known to other mountaineers, such as deer and wild sheep, who paw out oval hollows and lie beneath the larger trees in safe and comfortable concealment."

Whitebark Pine male cones

Whitebark Pine female cones

Whitebark Pines

Plants Cover the Hillsides in a Rainbow of Color

After leaving the shoreline of Frog Lake, the trail soon arrives at gardens that burst into color in July while distant Caples Lake can be seen in the distance. These wild gardens are a photographer's and botanist's paradise with creeks that seep down the hillsides to support a wide variety of flowers. Among them are lupines, butterweeds, and the Mountain Bluebells (*Mertensia ciliata*), which grows 3–4' tall with fragrant flowers that are pink in bud and blue in bloom.

Lupines and Butterweeds

While standing in these colorful gardens and looking out over the flowers, it's amazing to realize how much cooperation there is in this diverse, complex community. Flowers, birds, and insects sustain life in one another through the exchange of pollen and nectar. Trees and other plants absorb carbon dioxide from the air and release oxygen back into it in a balance that sustains our lives and the lives of all other animals. Trees and shrubs shelter insects, birds, and animals, and they draw up water from the soil into

Mountain Bluebells

Cooperative coummunity of flowers

their leaves, which is then released back into the soil through evaporation. All plants help to retain the fertile soils by preventing or reducing erosion with their extensive root systems. Leaves live in a cooperative relationship with chloroplasts, which they house while the chloroplasts manufacture the life-sustaining carbohydrates that sustain their plants and other forms of life. Massive networks of soil fungi cover the root tips of conifers and other plants, cooperatively enabling plants to live in nitrogen deficient soils, while the plants that photosynthesize produce the carbohydrates that feed the fungi.

Anna's Hummingbird on Anderson's Thistle

Cooperative relationships have evolved over millions of years into amazing partnerships. Within the insect world, one of the most astounding examples is between ants and aphids. Ants stroke the backs of "their" aphids to induce them to produce a sweet substance, called "honeydew." This substance has the exact balance of carbohydrates, amino acids, and water that the ants require. In exchange, the ants hover over and protect the aphids from predators and shield them from the weather. Some ants actually herd their aphids into their ant nests when the weather is harsh, or they create mud huts with their saliva and soil and herd the aphids into them for protection. Other ants gather their aphids' eggs and take them into their ant hills for the winter. Come spring, they return the aphid eggs to plants near the ant hills to hatch.

In his book *Peaceable Nature*, Stephan Lackner found from his studies in Africa that animals cooperate far more than they compete and that they live their lives in relative harmony with approximately 95% dying from natural causes rather than from predation. On the Galapagos Islands, Darwin discovered nature maintaining its equilibrium and healthy, balanced functioning with few predators and with cooperation as the norm.

In his book *Restoring the Soul of the World, Our Living Bond with Nature's Intelligence*, David Fideler writes that we need to heal the ecosystems that we have damaged by respecting and supporting nature's own regenerative abilities. He writes, "The natural world can regnerate itself in much shorter periods of time than anyone thought possible. This regeneration occurs not through a process of technological control, but through a living partnership in which we are able to hear, learn from, and actively collaborate with nature's intelligence and the living world."

Wandering in Creekside Gardens

As you continue along the trail, you'll cross a creek where you can look for the pink flowers of **Elephant's Head** that delight both children and adults. Once I was hiking at Tahoe, when a darling little girl, about 7 years old, appeared and began walking beside me. As we were chatting about the plants she said, "You know, I have a thing about nature!!!" I was delighted and said, "Well, I have a thing about nature too!" I shared the names of Elephant's Heads, Monkeyflowers, and Caterpillar Phacelias with her. She giggled with delight at each new, funny name. Nature nourishes all little children who find delight in outdoor play, and they nurture us with their joy and wide-open hearts.

Elephant's Head

Nature's fun

Elephant's Head flowers resemble tiny, rounded foreheads of pink elephants with floppy ears and upturned trunks. If you gently lift the trunk, you'll find its reproductive parts hidden inside, and you might wonder how insects pollinate the flowers. Bees buzz-pollinate these plants by holding onto their flowers and vibrating their wings so rapidly that they cause the pollen inside the flower to be released onto their bodies, which they then carry to other Elephant's Head flowers. **Little Elephant's Head** grows in the same wet habitats but are smaller and less elephant-head-like with their tiny, curled trunks.

If you see deep pink flowers high above the trail, climb up the hillside to enjoy the Sierra Primroses, but be careful as you climb the hillside in boggy areas by walking on rocks when possible. Small plants in such areas are easily damaged by many boots. Also look by the hillside creeks for **Sierra Claytonia** with fleshy leaves and white to pink flowers. Five anthers surround the ovary and stigma, and yellow spots mark the base of the petals, put-

Little Elephant's Head

ting on quite a show for insects. At the base of the petals are what look like speckles of sugar to cleverly attract pollinators.

Sierra Claytonia

Tanya Aminoff

Creekside Marsh Marigolds (*Caltha leptosepala*) bloom in June, with white, petal-like sepals and yellow pistils. Later, the delicate flowers of **Brook Saxifrage** bloom on 8–20" tall, naked, finely haired stems with basal, rounded, and lobed leaves. Its tiny flowers are exquisite through a hand lens and seem to float on their delicate stems. Its white petals are yellow-spotted and their anthers are red and are supported by fleshy filaments. As their seeds mature, the ovaries turn red resembling tiny bird beaks.

Marsh Marigold

Spending Time Alone

While in these gardens, wander off to find a special place where you can sit down to be alone with the flowers. Allow your mind to quiet down and sink into the beauty and rich aliveness surrounding you. It's mind boggling when we stop to truly experience the flowers, these exquisite, intricate beings who have been evolving for 450 million years. It was the energy of their pollen that gave rise to the development of warm-blooded animals, by providing the energy they needed to maintain their body warmth in the cold.

Lisa Berry

Brook Saxifrage and its flower

Flowers are millions of tiny miracles and "gifts from the Gods" that we get to experience every day. Perhaps sometimes we take them for granted, but what would our lives be without the beauty of flowers? What if the whole world were just made up of green and brown plants, without a touch of color anywhere? When we take time to slow down and actually stop, we aren't just looking *at* flowers, we are actually seeing into them with our hearts. George Washington Carver, who went out every morning in the woods by his home to

Time alone in the flowers

Monument Plant

Monument Plant flowers

Monument Plant flower closeup

Monument Plant leaves before the stalk appears

talk with the flowers, once said, "When I touch a flower, I am not merely touching that flower. I am touching infinity." So lie back now and spend time touching infinity with your heart and soul. Empty your mind. If it is a warm day, let the sun bathe your body with its delicious warmth as the flowers and leaves sweeten you with their fragrance.

As the trail continues toward Winnemucca Lake, you'll be in vast open country, enjoying the fragrance of Tahoe's pure air, and you'll see the startling **Monument Plant** or Green Gentian towering over the other plants on the hillsides. Its white to green petals are spotted, and white fringe decorates the purple nectar glands. Their stamens spread outward with yellow anthers, and the swollen green pistil sits "enthusiastically" in the center, topped with a short style and rounded stigma. Before the plant produces its tall stalk and flowers, it forms a cluster of large leaves that are like no other plant. This plant used to be considered a biennial, until Dr. David Inouye of the Rocky Mountain Biological Laboratory in Colorado, who has been studying it since the 1960s, found that a microscopic flower stalk begins forming 3–4 years before the visible stalk appears. After living for an average of 30 to 40 years, or even up to 80 years in some cases, the plant bursts into flower once and then sets seed and dies.

Arriving at Winnemucca Lake

Soon Winnemucca Lake comes into view, dramatically backdropped by Round Top Mountain. Historical accounts say the lake was named after the Paiute Chief Winnemucca (1820–1882) and his daughter Sara Winnemucca

(~1844–1891). She became well known and respected for her leadership, intelligence, and her nationally recognized campaign to gain rights for her people. She was fluent in Spanish, English, and several indigenous languages and worked as an interpreter just as her grandfather, Truckee, had done. She was committed to bringing peace between the settlers and her people and tells her story in her book, *Life Among the Paiutes, Their Wrongs and Claims*.

Western Prickly Gooseberry

In the conifer understory near the lake, you'll find Western Prickly Gooseberry (*Ribes montigenum*), a shrub found at high elevations that grows from 2–4' tall. Its five tiny, reddish petals sit at the base of larger, creamy colored sepals. The green swelling below the sepals is the ovary, with glandular bristles on its surface, that becomes orange-red, bristled, sweet fruit that is relished by birds and other animals. Its maple-like leaves are lobed and covered with fragrant, glandular hairs. You'll also see the 3–4' tall shrubs of Labrador Tea blooming at the lake's edge with white flowers and extended stamens.

Mountain Heather

Other treasures found here include the low shrubs of Cassiope (*Cassiope mertensiana*) with red-capped sepals and white, bell-shaped flowers that nod on red stems. Their tightly packed leaves are overlapping and fleshy. The pink, fuzzy-looking flowers of Mountain Heather (*Phyllodoce breweri*) grow on evergreen shrubs with leaves that resemble small pine needles. Its reproductive parts are easily seen without a hand lens. The pistil sits in the flower's center with a yellow ovary and a pink style that rises out of the ovary with a rounded stigma. Pink stamens whorl outward from the ovary supporting pollen-bearing, pink anthers.

A day spent by these beautiful lakes will leave you with an experience you'll never forget. Though this trail is popular and usually crowded with many people, these pristine lakes can feel isolated, if you find a secret place along their shorelines and tuck yourself into a clump of trees, hidden in your own little bit of heaven.

#19 Meiss Meadow Trail past Red Lake Peak

Red Lake Peak from Hwy 88

👢 👢 👢 👢

One Way: 3 miles
Trail Begins/Ends: 8,400'/8,500'
Map: AM: Lake Tahoe Basin
Wildflower Season: mid May through August

Red Lake Peak appears barren and imposing from Highway 88 near 8,574' Carson Pass, but on the trail this first impression is quickly forgotten among the wildflowers and massive Junipers that rise among immense boulders. In early June, the flower season begins with Spring Beauty, Steer's Head, and Beckwith's Violet. In June and July, brightly colored lupines, Mule's Ears, and Western Wall Flowers decorate the slopes. Breathtaking mountain vistas appear along the uphill climb as the trail crests an 8,880' saddle and then reaches a pond and large meadow of purple irises. The trail ends by flowery Meiss Meadow by the headwaters of the Upper Truckee River.

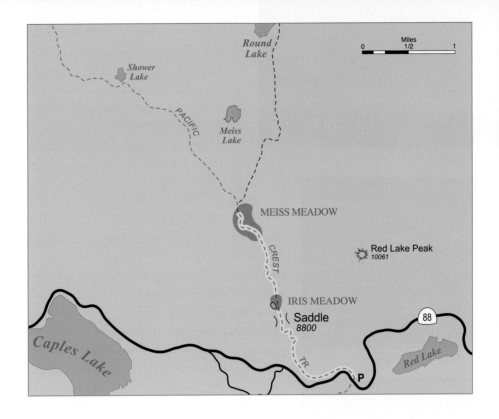

Featured Flowers

Steer's Head (*Dicentra uniflora*)
Spring Beauty (*Claytonia lanceolata*)
Bog Mallow (*Sidalcea oregana*)
Western Blue Flag (*Iris missouriensis*)
Prairie Smoke (*Geum triflorum*)
Beckwith's Violet (*Viola beckwithii*)

Trailhead Directions: **Take Highway 88** to the Carson Pass Visitor's Center where you can learn about Kit Carson's travels through the Sierra and see the stone monolith honoring Snowshoe Thompson. Then drive 0.2 mile west on Hwy 88 to the Meiss Meadow Trailhead parking on the east side of the road. There is a fee to park, which is waived with a Golden Age pass.

The trail begins by a small creek with Plantain Buttercups (*Ranunculus alismifolius*) that bloom in June. They are named for their shiny, yellow petals, a shininess caused by light reflected off a layer of white starch grains below the yellow pigment cells. Also at the trail's beginning under the conifers, you'll

Trailhead meadow of Plantain Buttercups

Woolly-flowered Gooseberry

Sierra Juniper on the trail and its female cones

find the spreading, 3' tall shrubs of Woolly-flowered Gooseberry (*Ribes lasianthum*). Its small, yellow flowers shelter tiny, white anthers that peek out from the petals. Later, glabrous, red berries appear.

The trail continues through a Red Fir, Lodgepole Pine, and Juniper forest with dramatic rock walls and gardens of Wandering Daisies, Sulphur Flowers, Mountain Pennyroyals, and other flowers. Soon, it reaches Quaking Aspens and crosses slabs of granite where Sierra Junipers (*Juniperus grandis*) sit wedged between granite boulders like regal patriarchs. John Muir described the Juniper as "a thickset, sturdy, picturesque highlander seemingly content to live for more than a score of centuries on sunshine and snow; a truly wonderful fellow, dogged endurance expressed in every feature, lasting about as long as the granite he stands on." Junipers grow up to 10,000' elevations. They can live for a thousand years and reach heights of 100'. At high, wind swept elevations, they may only grow to a stunted 10' rising on tenaciously clinging root systems that form a stable platform to spend their lives in stoic defiance of the harsh elements. Native Americans placed their sticky, blue seed cones near anthills. After the ants consumed the sweet substance from the center of the fleshy cones, the cones were strung and dried to make fragrant, berry-beaded necklaces.

As the trail continues to climb, there are views toward Elephant's Back (9,585'), Round Top Mountain (10,381'), and Caples Lake. The highway noise fades away among the Scarlet Gilias, Alpine Asters, and Sierra Onions. When the trail re-enters a forest, if you are here in late May to early June, look for the grayish green, divided leaves and small, unusual flowers of **Steer's Head** that rise only a few inches off the ground. Each flower is a tiny replica of a sun-bleached steer's head that eerily rests on desert floors. "Dicentra" refers to its 2-spurred flower and "uniflora" is for its single flower per stem. Their small, ground carpeting leaves are easy to miss, but once you spot them, you'll find so many plants that you'll wonder how you could have missed them. The delicate flowers of **Spring Beauty** grow in the forest nearby with charming, white to pink, striped blossoms with pink anthers and narrow, lance-shaped leaves. This early bloomer also announces the arrival of spring.

Steer's Head

Spring Beauty

Hillside Flowers

Soon the trail crosses a creek with a garden of cinquefoils, monkeyflowers, columbines, ferns, and willows. After passing several creeks, the trail begins a gradual climb up switchbacks on a vast, open hillside. In June violets, onions, and locoweeds bloom, followed by lupines, Mule's Ears, and Woolly Sunflowers. The 2′ tall Western Wallflower (*Erysimum capitatum*) brightens the hillsides with its fragrant, yellow flowers. Later its seeds mature into long, thin, flattened pods. The 4–12″ tall

Western Wallflower

Sierra Onion

Dwarf Onion

Pursh's Woolly Pod

Lance-leaf Stonecrop

Sierra Onion (*Allium campanulatum*) blooms with pink flowers, and the ground-hugging Dwarf Onion (*Allium obtusum*) grows with curling leaves surrounding its creamy colored, reddish to brown striped flowers. The cutest little flower is Pursh's Woolly Pod (*Astragalus purshii*) with vivid rosy purple pea flowers, hairy leaves, and fuzzy white pea pods.

In July, the dry habitat Lance-leaf Stonecrop (*Sedum lanceolatum*) blooms on 8″ tall stems with yellow, star-shaped flowers above succulent leaves. Stonecrops are interesting, because they carry out photosynthesis through an unusual process called "Crassulacean Acid Metabolism" (CAM). It's complicated, but to simplify it . . . during photosynthesis most plants take up water and minerals through their roots and absorb carbon dioxde (CO_2) from the air during the day through their leaf stomata. "Stomata," which is Greek for "mouths," are tiny mouth-shaped pores in leaves that open and close to take in the CO_2. With the energy of sunlight, their leaves then combine these substances to create the carbohydrates plants need to survive, and oxygen is produced as a by-product.

Since photosynthesis requires the energy of sunlight, most plants open their stomata during the day to absorb sunlight and CO_2 and to transpire water off the leaves. They then close the stomata at night to prevent water from evaporating off the leaves, when they aren't photosynthesizing. Sedums evolved to do the opposite. They open their stomata at night, instead of during the day, to absorb the CO_2. Since water vapor evaporates more slowly during the night in the cooler temperatures, they can minimize their water loss, which is important in such dry habitats. They can do this, because unlike other plants they have an enzyme in their leaves that has a high affinity for CO_2 that enables sedums to store the carbon in their leaves during the night. As the next day heats up, they minimize the opening of their stomata and reduce water loss, while they photosynthesize in the sunlight with the stored CO_2. Stonecrops also survive in dry habitats by storing water in their thick, succulent leaves to draw upon when water is scarce.

Reaching the Saddle

After climbing up the switchbacks, the trail reaches an 8,800′ saddle 1.2 miles from the trailhead. While there, take some time to find a comfortable place to lie back and enjoy the flowers and fabulous mountain scenery. John Muir experienced a similar sight in Yosemite, "How boundless the sky seems as we revel in these storm-beaten sky gardens amid so vast a congregation of on-looking mountains. Strange and admirable it is that the more savage and chilly and storm-chafed the mountains, the finer the glow on their faces and the finer the plants they bear. The myriads of flowers tinging the mountain-top do not seem to have grown out of the dry, rough gravel of disintegration, but rather they appear as visitors, a cloud of witnesses to Nature's love . . . every flower a window opening into heaven, a mirror reflecting the Creator."

Once, I hiked to this saddle when a wild storm suddenly began to blow in. Soon streaks of lightning sparked across the darkened sky, heavy rain began drenching me, and the winds that gusted across the mountainside were so powerful, I felt I could be blown off the exposed ridgeline at any moment. While it was scary, it was also exhilarating to be in the midst of such wild power. As I scurried down the mountain, I was ecstatic and filled with gratitude to be enveloped by the storm's intense energy.

A Pond by Pink Mallows and Lavender Iris

Your experience may be calmer and, after relaxing, you only have a short walk to the pond where Red Lake Peak looms into view by a meadow of

Pond by the Western Blue Flag irises

June blooming Bog Mallows and irises. The pink flowered **Bog Mallow** grows in the meadow on 6–12″ tall stems. Its small, Hollyhock-like flowers grow in clustered spikes, and its round, scalloped-edged leaves are mainly basal. The 2′ tall iris, **Western Blue Flag**, grows nearby with flowers composed of three blue- to purple-striped, white petal-like sepals. The sepals bend downward providing a pathway for pollinators seeking nectar at their base. The female, petal-like styles are the structures in between the sepals and upright blue-purple petals. The stigma and stamen are attached to the bottom of each style.

Bog Mallow and its flower

The iris pollination process is extraordinary. Bees are attracted to the large, colorful, landing-pad sepals and are guided along them by the blue and golden nectar lines. As a bee enters the flower with pollen she has gathered from another iris, she walks along the sepal under the stigma toward the nectar. In doing so, she pushes the stigma, which is above her, down and backward and exposes the stigma's receptive tip. This action causes her to dust the stigma with pollen and pollinate the flower. As she backs out after sipping the nectar, she unrolls the bent-back stigma, causing the stigma's receptive part to now face upward and away from her, which prevents her from pollinating the stigma with the flower's own pollen. This process is truly extraordinary, but then so is all life.

Red Lake Peak Beckons

Western Blue Flag

As you stand in the meadow by the irises, you'll be looking toward Red Lake Peak. From its 10,061′ peak, John Fremont and Charles Preuss made the first recorded sighting of Lake Tahoe on Valentine's Day, 1844. After a hard climb up through deep snow, they crested the mountain and saw the lake below. That evening, Fremont took out his journal and wrote, "We had a beautiful view of a mountain lake at our feet, about fifteen miles in length, and so entirely surrounded by mountains that we could not discover an outlet." Much has changed in the world since Fremont reached the peak that day, and yet on the mountain's flank, little has changed. The flowers still bloom year after year as they have done for thousands of years.

To hike up to the alpine summit of Red Lake Peak, you'll need to start up the mountain from its west side across the highway from Carson Pass, but to see the mountain's flowers blooming on its flanks in June through July, head cross-country through the iris meadow as far as you want up the mountain. Violets, gilias, lupines and sunflowers bloom in purples, pinks, reds, and yellows on low growing cushion plants and taller plants that are adapted to the mountain's windy habitat.

Woolly Groundsel

You'll find lots of woolly haired plants seeking protection from the wind and intense solar rays as they hunker down in the rocks. Look for more rosy purple flowered Woolly Pods and the yellow flowered Woolly Groundsel, which grows 6" tall above downy, white basal leaves. You'll find Whitney's Locoweed with purple or white flowers and red striped, inflated fruit. Timberline Phacelia grows with white or lavender flowers

Timberline Phacelia

on caterpillar-like coils above its silver, densely hairy, prominently veined leaves. You'll also find Gordon's Ivesia, which blooms with yellow flowers that cluster on top of 6" long stems. Woolly Sunflowers brighten their rocky habitats with yellow. The sweet, daisy flowers of Shining Fleabane

Woolly Sunflowers

Shining Fleabane

Dwarf Everlasting

bloom with lavender or white flowers and turn blue as they age. Other plants don't grow low to the ground, like the pink and red Sky Rockets, yellow Wallflowers, Whorled and Showy Penstemons, and the gracefully drooping flowers of Blue Flax. The least showy plant of all is the ground hugging Dwarf Everlasting that blooms early in June with 1" tall stems on the mountain's flank and on the slopes above the pond. Check the "Flowers by Color" section to help you identify these flowers.

Prairie Smoke and its fruit

When you return to the trail, you'll find **Prairie Smoke** blooming in June to early July. It grows up to 12" tall with small, creamy colored, reddish-pink-tinged flowers with maroon or reddish sepals. After fertilization, its bell-shaped flowers turn upward, and the petals and sepals fall off exposing swelling seeds that are topped with 1½" long, feathery styles. Nearby will be California Hesperochiron (*Hesperochiron californicus*), a low growing plant with white to pale pink flowers. Its basal leaves are hairy, and the flower is tubular with flaring petals. A surprise in late May to early June are the hundreds of **Beckwith's Violets** that bloom with lovely purple petals and yellow throats. Their dull green, deeply dissected leaves are not the usual violet leaf. Be sure to kneel down to enjoy the beauty of their sweet little faces and to grace them with your presence.

Beckwith's Violets

A Curious Squirrel

As you walk along the trail, keep your ears and eyes open for Belding's Ground Squirrel, a cute animal that might curiously walk out onto the trail to check you out. It makes its home in burrows in sagebrush flats and damp meadows from 6,000' to 12,000' and mainly feeds on flowers and seeds but also consumes bulbs, mushrooms, and insects. Ground Squirrels don't cache their food; instead they eat almost constantly when their hibernation time draws near and then depend upon the fat they've built up to last through their long 8–9 month hibernation. In early spring, females and males come out to mate, and the females begin digging their nesting burrows and line them with grasses. They give

Belding's Ground Squirrel

birth to 3–8 young, usually around June in the higher country, and they care for them alone until they emerge again from their burrows for the summer.

Continuing to Meiss Meadow

The trail to Meiss Meadow offers views of Lake Tahoe and at small creek crossing, many intense displays of Large-leaf Lupines in July. In the distance you'll see flowers cascading down a large canyon. After this, the trail

Creek crossing with Large-leaf Lupines

Canyon flowers from Meiss Meadow Trail

Brewer's Cinquefoil

Brewer's Cinquefoil

descends, and you'll head into a conifer forest with a meadow of Wandering Daisies.

When the trail enters damp meadows, look for Brewer's Cinquefoil (*Potentilla breweri*). Its bright yellow, 5-petaled flowers are 2-lobed at the tip and are striking against its white-haired green leaves. It grows upright and as a low-growing mat with leaves that are pinnate. The leaflets are palmately lobed and overlapping. "Cinquefoil" is derived from a combination of old English, French, and Latin words. "Cinque" for "five" and "foil" for "leaf" means "five leaflets." "Potentilla" means "little powerful one" for the medicinal use of a European species. The genus *Potentilla* is divided into 300 species worldwide.

The trail seems to go on forever, through various meadows, before large, beautiful, 8,400′ Meiss Meadow is reached. The Meiss family cabin and barn is by the headwaters of the Upper Truckee River. Interpretive panels tell the story of the family. Evelyn Meiss Richard remembers her childhood summers spent in Meiss Meadow, ". . . My three sisters and I had many a lovely summer fishing and riding horseback. Once a week some of us would ride our horses to Meyers to pick up our mail. It took us most of the day for the trip. My mother, in the meantime, would either make ice cream to be frozen in the snow bank, or bread and biscuits in the wood stove."

In July and August, the large meadow is covered with Elephant's Heads, paintbrushes, lupines, butterweeds, monkeyflowers, and other flowers. One of the most abundant flowers is the blue to purple Whorled Penstemon (*Penstemon hetero-*

Meiss Meadow Barn

doxus). It creates an expanse of vibrant color throughout the meadow in July. It is a joy to linger here for a picnic by the creek and to wander among the flowers. If you leave the meadow in late afternoon as the sun is dropping, the flowers along the trail will be backlit and glow with new delight in a dazzling display to guide you happily back to your car.

Meiss Meadow flowers

#20 Woods Lake to Winnemucca & Round Top Lakes

Round Top Mountain

🥾 🥾 🥾 🥾

One Way: 3 miles
Trail Begins/Ends: 8,200'/9,400'
Map: AM: Lake Tahoe Basin
Wildflower Season: June through September

Winnemucca and Round Top Lakes are reached after a gradual uphill climb through the filtered light of a forest and after passing a vast, bowl-shaped valley with magnificent wildflowers in July and August. A cascading creek in the valley flows over boulders with great delight, nourishing lush flower gardens. All this beauty is backdropped by powerful Round Top Mountain overlooking the valley like a welcoming, beneficent Being. On the grassy banks of both lakes, rugged Whitebark Pines extend their branches with gifts of resiny seed cones, while the penetrating call of a Clark's Nutcracker echoes through the trees. The windswept trail to Round Top Lake blooms abundantly with special alpine plants.

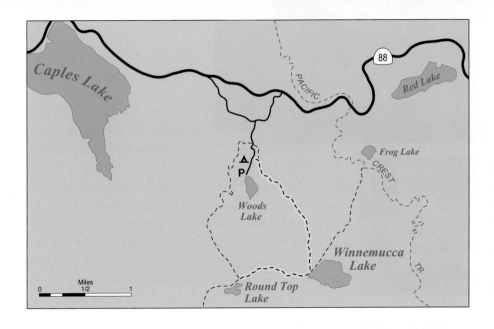

Featured Flowers
Cassiope (*Cassiope mertensiana*)
Bog Laurel (*Kalmia polifolia*)
Showy Polemonium (*Polemonium pulcherrimum*)
Alpine Buttercup (*Ranunculus eschscholtzii*)
Alpine Shooting Star (*Primula tetranda*)
Western Pasque Flower (*Anemone occidentalis*)

Trailhead Directions: **The trailhead is off Highway 88**, 1.7 miles west from Carson Pass on the south side of the highway or about **3 miles east of Caples Lake**. After turning off the highway, drive over the cement bridge and head 0.4 mile to the day parking by Woods Lake. Ignore the "Winnemucca Lake 2½ miles" sign, just after the bridge. That is for the west side of a loop; we'll take the dramatic, east side of the loop. A good campground is passed before the day parking. The $5 parking fee, waived with a Golden Age Pass, can be purchased in the parking area or at the trailhead. Be prepared for this high-elevation hike with warm clothing. In summer a freezing, wet storm can blow in.

The trail begins by the trailhead sign and wooden bridge that was passed before the parking lot at Woods Lake. With young children, this can be a short 0.5-mile hike to enjoy the valley flowers and creek. On the bridge over the lower part of the creek, you'll pass Mountain Alders (*Alnus incana*) with

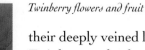

Twinberry flowers and fruit

their deeply veined leaves and Twinberry shrubs (*Lonicera involucrata*) with yellow, tubular flowers or black fruit surrounded by red bracts.

At the trail split just after the bridge, head right through a rocky habitat of Pussytoes, Mountain Heathers, and Mountain Pride past large boulders that are fun for little people. Soon the trail enters a forest of Hemlocks, and Lodgepole, Jeffrey, and Western White Pines. Jacob's Ladder (*Polemonium californicum*) grows at the base of conifers with blue flowers enclosing white stamens and a curled stigma. Its leaves are pinnate on vertical and spreading stems.

Boulder fun for little ones

Reaching the Flowered Valley

In about 0.5 mile from the trailhead, you'll reach the valley, which generally is in peak bloom by mid July through August. In its lush gardens along the trail, Giant Red Paintbrush, Arrowleaf Butterweed, Narrow-tube Sky Rocket bloom by Sticky Cinquefoils (*Drymocallis glandulosa*). This Cinquefoil grows up to 2½' tall with yellow or creamy white flowers. Its leaves are pinnate and were brewed into a tea by Native Americans to treat stomach pain and headaches.

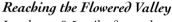

Jacob's Ladder

Trail past Lupine and Paintbrush

Sticky Cinquefoil

You'll also see many Large-leaf Lupines (*Lupinus polyphyllus*). They grow 3–5′ tall with blue to purplish flowers above palmate leaves that have 5–11 leaflets. Take a moment to see if bees are visiting the lupines. Female bees pollinate its flowers, and it is fun to watch as they fly onto the flower's keel. Their tiny bit of weight pushes the keel down, which releases the flower's style to pop up and expose its receptive stigma to be dusted with pollen from the bee's body. If there are no bees, gently push down the keel's tip to see its reproductive parts pop up.

Large-leaf Lupine

Look at several lupine flowers, and you'll notice that some have a white spot on the banner petal, and others have a dark purplish spot. Do you know why the spots differ . . . something very interesting has happened! This little flower changes its white banner spot to a dark one on pollinated flowers to direct pollinators to its un-pollinated, white spotted flowers. Bees have learned that petals with contrasting spots, lines, and colors lead to sweet nectar, and since their vision differs from ours, they don't see any contrast on the lupine's dark spotted flowers. Though they also pollinate flowers without contrasting marks, bees know that lupines with white spots yield what they are seeking.

Steve Ashcraft

Bee pollinating the Tahoe Lupine

In dry habitats, you'll find the blue Tahoe Lupine (*Lupinus argenteus* var. *meionanthus*). Its small, round-shaped flowers bloom above silvery haired, palmate leaves with 5–9 leaflets. It's the easiest lupine to identify, because its flowers are smaller than most other lupines, and its leaves are very white-silky. The purple Hoary Aster (*Dieteria canescens*) also grows in dry soil right along the trail. It is 4–20″ tall with leaves that may be linear to lance-like or oval. "Hoary" refers to the grey to white hairs on its phyllaries and is Latin for "hairy."

banner petal

wing petals

Typical Lupine flowers

Hoary Aster

The Boisterous Clark's Nutcracker

The trail passes more exuberant cascades and rocky habitats as it begins a steeper uphill climb toward Round Top Mountain and Winnemucca Lake. On the open conifer slopes, you'll likely hear Clark's Nutcracker, a bird

with a distinctive, loud "khaaa" cry. It feeds on seeds of the Whitebark Pine, a primitive pine that is unable to open its cones to release its seeds. Instead, it depends upon Nutcrackers or other animals to break the seeds free and then plant and distribute them.

Nutcrackers contain a special pouch under their tongues that can hold up to 150 seeds at a time. What isn't eaten right away is cached in holes they dig in the ground. In one season, they can collect up to 30,000 seeds and cache them in 10,000 locations over an area of 10 square miles! These extraordinary

Clark's Nutcracker

birds don't find their caches by smell. They extrapolated the location of each cache when they buried the seeds and later remember the locations of their caches. With a superb memory, they can return to the exact locations to find their caches, even after the seeds have been buried under snow. If their calculations are off by even a few inches, the seeds won't be found. I once watched a Nutcracker as it analyzed a small area on the ground from high up in conifer and then flew down to easily dig up its seeds. For some reason, my presence didn't disturb it.

Arriving at Winnemucca Lake

As the trail levels out 2 miles from the trailhead, you'll be in an open, exposed habitat by Winnemucca Lake. There you'll find a large variety of flowers, which are discussed on the Frog to Winnemucca Lake hike. One flower you don't want to miss is **Cassiope**, which grows 8–12″ tall and is found on the hill after the trail leaves the lake. Its nodding, red stemmed, white flowers are topped with tiny, red sepal caps. It's named for the Greek myth of Cassiopeia whose daughter was stolen and chained to a rock but later rescued. What this has to do with this lovely little flower, I can't imagine, except that it often grows among rocks. Rather than being chained to the rocks, it blooms lavishly around them, perhaps symbolizing the freeing of Cassiope's daughter.

Cassiope

John Muir searched a long time in Yosemite to find Cassiope, after which he exclaimed, "I met cassiope growing in fringes among the battered rocks. Her blossoms had faded long ago, but they were still clinging with happy memories to the evergreen sprays, and still so beautiful as to thrill every fiber of one's being . . . No evangel among all the mountain plants speaks Nature's love more plainly than cassiope."

Mountain Heather on Round Top Trail

Mountain Heather (*Phyllodoce breweri*) is a small shrub with deep pink flowers and long stamens, so the flowers appear fuzzy. Its needle-like leaves grow on 6–10″ tall stems. "Breweri" honors William Henry Brewer (1828–1910) who collected this Heather in Yosemite in 1863 as he traveled up California recording the state's flora, fauna, and geology for the Whitney Survey.

Mountain Heather

Heading to Round Top Lake

From Winnemucca Lake, you'll head west on an exposed, gradual, uphill climb past Spreading Phlox, Jewelflowers, sedums, wallflowers,

Enjoying Round Top Lake for early flowers

anther
pocket

released
anthers

Bog Laurel flowers and anthers

and Sulphur Flowers. Along the way, you'll cross a creek with Marsh Marigolds. After about 0.8 mile, the trail arrives at stark, beautiful Round Top Lake, where in June to early July, you'll be treated to some of Tahoe's best alpine flower displays. **Bog Laurel** covers areas of the lake's grassy shoreline with plants 4–10" tall. Its pink flowers support 10 thread-like filaments. Each filament carries a dark anther, which is tucked into a little pocket that holds down the anther until a bee lands on the flower. Her weight suddenly releases the anther from its pocket, and the anther springs up to dust her body with ripened pollen! This little plant doesn't waste any time making sure that bees gather its pollen. The Bog Laurel is beautiful in fall also, when its leaves turn brilliant red, decorating the lake's edge with its brilliance.

Be sure to walk around to the far side of the lake and up the rocky hillsides below the flanks of the two peaks called The Sisters (10,153′). Here the flowers may be so spectacular that you may

Showy Polemonium on slope below The Sisters

hear love-crazed botanists shouting with joy among the flowers! Gorgeous **Showy Polemonium** spreads over the bare soil on the flanks of The Sisters with yellow-centered, blue flowers. It grows in dense clumps up to 6–12″ tall and selects ridgetops and mountain summits to show off its beauty.

The **Alpine Buttercup** blooms close to the ground with bright yellow flowers and happy little faces that greet hikers. You'll also find blue Showy and Whorled Penstemons growing among the rocks near the lavender flowers of Dagger Pod, which form dagger-shaped fruits. If you keep your eyes open in the rocky area, you might even see a cute Short-tailed Weasel. This little animal is 7–12″ long and lives at high elevations in openings among the rocks. It is a fierce little carnivore that eats mice and voles. As winter approaches, weasels molt in response to the shortening day length by turning white for camouflage in the snow, although their tail tips remain black.

Alpine Buttercups

Lisa Berry

Short-tailed Weasel

Exploring Gardens West of the Lake

After returning to the trail, continue walking west, cross country, beyond the lake to explore meadows, forests, and rocky areas to find more fabulous alpine plants blooming from late May through July or even into August in a good snow year. In boggy areas, look for the **Alpine Shooting Star** with its beautiful, nodding, pink flowers with 4 petals. As its name suggests, it resembles stars that soar through the night sky with a tail of blazing light. Only the flower's "tail" is made up of 4 pink, reflexed petals. A single pistil hangs down and outward from its brown to black stamens. After fertilization, each nodding flower turns upward, as if to celebrate

Alpine Shooting Star

Dwarf Lewisia

Three-leaved Lewisia

Sibbaldia

Sierra Saxifrage

its fulfillment. The sepals, hidden until now by their reflexed petals, become visible as the petals fall off. The sepals then move upwards around the maturing seed capsule, like protective hands cradling a treasure.

Alpine Shooting Star was named *"Dodecatheon alpinum"* before it was recently moved to the *Primula* genus and named *"Primula tetranda."* Its old name, *"Dodecatheon"* is Greek for "dodeka" for "twelve" and "theos" for "gods." Pliny, a Roman naturalist and writer (23–79 A.D.), gave the plant this name, because its clusters of flowers, each bearing a crown of reflexed petals, reminded him of an assembly of the twelve important gods of the Roman world. Just think how long this lovely flower has been admired and cherished, though he most certainly wasn't the first to do so.

You'll also find the Dwarf Lewisia (*Lewisia pygmaea*) growing in grassy areas, only a few inches tall with white, pink-striped flowers that nestle in its fleshy leaves. The similar looking Three-leaved Lewisia (*Lewisia triphylla*) grows nearby with white, pink-striped flowers also. It usually has 3 very narrow, fleshy leaves per stem, but there can be fewer or more leaves. Nevada Lewisia (*Lewisia nevadensis*) is found nearby growing 1–3″ tall with many petaled, white flowers and fleshy leaves.

Also in moist areas, look for the 1–4″ tall Sibbaldia (*Sibbaldia procumbens*) with stems that support three wedge-shaped, toothed leaflets. Its green sepals are larger than its tiny yellow petals. In damp, grassy areas, Sierra Saxifrage (*Micranthes aprica*) grows about 6″ tall with small, densely clustered flowers on solitary stems. Its petals are very tiny and separate. The anthers are golden to reddish, and the ovary forms two red beaks as their seeds mature and swell. The leaves are oval and are in a basal rosette.

Two species of the Rose Family are in the same area. Gordon's Ivesia (*Ivesia gordonii*) grows up to 10″ tall with yellow flowers on red, naked stems.

Its flowers support 2–4 pistils and 5 stamens. Club-moss Ivesia (*Ivesia lycopodioides*) is similar, but it is prostrate with yellow flowers also on naked, red stems. Its flowers differ with 5–15 pistils and 5 stamens.

Western Pasque Flower is a showy plant 6–18″ tall and is found in drying areas near the conifers. Its 2″ wide flowers are made up of white, petal-like sepals. As is typical in the Buttercup Family, it lacks true petals, but pollinators are attracted to its white sepals instead. Each hairy stem supports one flower, and its fluffy, shaggy haired leaves are deeply divided. The hairy, pink-edged flowers are cute as they emerge in a leafy cup in spring. The Pasque Flower is infrequent at Tahoe, so it's very special to find them growing so abundantly here. After pollination the feathery styles cluster together above the seeds and form floppy looking "muppet heads."

The shaggiest plant of all in grassy meadows is Lyall's Dwarf Lupine (*Lupinus lepidus* var. *lobbii*), which was called Lyall's Lupine, until it was considered one of six varieties of *Lupinus lepidus*. This variety, "lobbii," grows up to an elevation of 10,500′ with small, soft hairy

Gordon's Ivesia

Club-moss Ivesia

Pasque flowers in early spring

Pasque Flower "muppet heads" in fruit

Western Pasque Flower

Lyall's Dwarf Lupine

leaves and blue pea flowers marked with a white spot on the banner petal. Do you see flowers that have darkened their white banner spot? If you can, you know why! Also check out its hairy leaves with your hand lens. Hairs on plants vary greatly, so it's interesting to look at all types of hairs on different plants. Some hairs are matted like a woolly sweater, others are long and soft, and others have tiny, star-shaped hairs at their tip. Some have sticky, glandular hairs with what looks like a drop of liquid at the top.

The plants that grow on this trail offer some of the most beautiful and abundant flower displays in all of Tahoe, so come here and immerse yourself in their beauty, a beauty that will stay with you for a long time afterwards or most likely for a lifetime.

Whitebark Pine endures the elements

#21 Thunder Mountain

Thunder Mountain Trail to the gap

One Way: 4.25 miles
Trail Begins/Ends: 7,980'/9,408'
Map: NG: Crystal Basin Silver Fork
Wildflower Season: May through August

Thunder Mountain hides behind a dark, dramatic ridgeline of jagged pinnacles that beckons hikers to its 9,408' summit. At the trail's beginning, small orchids bloom in a dark Red Fir forest. On open, wind-swept hillsides an array of colorful flowers bloom and at the highest elevations, cushion plants hug the ground creating dazzling displays among the rocks. For much of the hike, distant mountain vistas add to the beauty. The final climb to the mountaintop ends at an exhilarating "top of the world" perch with a spectacular 360-degree panorama of the Northern and Southern Sierra.

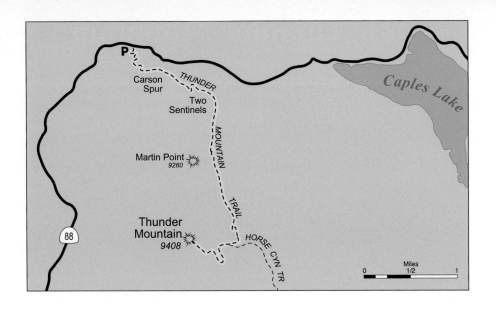

Featured Flowers

Spotted Coralroot Orchid (*Corallorhiza maculata*)
Dagger Pod (*Phoenicaulis cheiranthoides*)
Blue Fax (*Linum lewisii*)
Mount Rose Wild Buckwheat (*Eriogonum rosense*)
Woolly Groundsel (*Packera cana*)
Dwarf Monkeyflower (*Mimulus nanus* var. *mephiticus*)

Trailhead Directions: The Trailhead is 7.2 miles west of Carson Pass on Highway 88 and is on the south side of the highway. The trail follows exposed, windswept ridgelines with a mostly steady uphill climb, so this hike is for experienced hikers who are acclimated and in good shape or for those whose enthusiasm will spur them onward. I have found no springs or creeks along the trail to refill a water bottle. Storms can suddenly blow in and become dangerous at such high elevations, so come well prepared for changeable weather.

The trail begins in a forest of Lodgepole Pines, Western White Pines, and Red Firs and soon passes a small, wet meadow of Corn Lilies and Mule's Ears. Within about 200', you'll arrive at a trail post for Martin Meadow to the left and Thunder Mountain straight ahead. In the forest, keep your eyes open for the reddish **Spotted Coralroot Orchid**, which is easily missed since it blends with the brown forest duff. It grows up to 18" tall with small flowers, each with a white, red-spotted, lower petal. Because these orchids lack green leaves, they don't photosynthesize, and because they lack true roots, they depend upon soil fungi to survive. The fungi attach themselves to the orchid's coral-like, thick rhizomes and function as its roots and rootlets. The fungi absorb moisture and minerals from the soil, and they also attach themselves to the roots of nearby trees to absorb their carbon and nutrients. The fungi then attach themselves to the orchid's rhizomes to sustain these plants.

Coralroot Orchid

After a steady uphill climb through the trees, the trail enters an open slope with Sagebrush, Snowberry, Bitterbrush, and Pinemat Manzanita. At the top of the slope on the Carson Spur, you'll see a snow fence that was built to prevent large snow buildups and avalanches from falling down onto Highway 88. Here in June and July, Mule's Ears, Wavy-leaved Paintbrushes, *Calochortus* lilies, Scarlet Gilias, and Pennyroyals bloom alongside the lavender to blue flowers of the Spurred Lupine (*Lupinus argenteus* var. *heteranthus*). "Lupine" is from the Latin "lupus" for "wolf." Since lupines often grow in depleted soils, they were named with the assumption that they devour the soil's nutrients, like a wolf devours its food. Instead, the reverse is true. Lupines are nitrogen-fixing plants that house bacteria in small swellings on their roots. Bacteria "fix" or take in nitrogen from the air in the soil and convert it into a plant-usable form. Lupines and other members of the Pea Family enrich soils for other plants also, after the lupines die and decompose.

Spurred Lupine

As the trail continues, you'll begin to see glimpses of the imposing, lichen-covered, volcanic formations of the Two Sentinels (8780'), which appear beyond an impressive, 9' diameter Juniper. The trail soon leads back into the trees and up switchbacks past Western Sweet Cicely (*Osmorhiza occidentalis*). It grows from 1–3' tall

Western Sweet Cicely

Lemmon's Catchfly

Scarlet Gilia

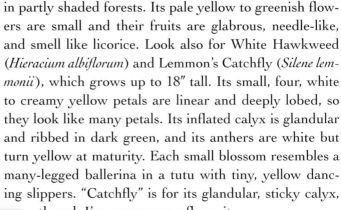

*Tahoe Lupine
and its flower's
shaggy "chin"*

in partly shaded forests. Its pale yellow to greenish flowers are small and their fruits are glabrous, needle-like, and smell like licorice. Look also for White Hawkweed (*Hieracium albiflorum*) and Lemmon's Catchfly (*Silene lemmonii*), which grows up to 18″ tall. Its small, four, white to creamy yellow petals are linear and deeply lobed, so they look like many petals. Its inflated calyx is glandular and ribbed in dark green, and its anthers are white but turn yellow at maturity. Each small blossom resembles a many-legged ballerina in a tutu with tiny, yellow dancing slippers. "Catchfly" is for its glandular, sticky calyx, though I've never seen a fly on it.

The trail leads to large, open, flowery slopes that rise up to the Sentinels and to views of Carson Pass, Kirkwood meadow, and distant mountains. In June and July, you'll find Sulphur Flower, Frosted Wild Buckwheat, Sagebrush, Whitney's Locoweed, and the bright red flowers of the 1–3′ tall, Scarlet Gilia (*Ipomopsis aggregata*). Its showy, tubular flowers and spotted petals attract hummingbirds, which pollinate their flowers. The birds probe the flower tubes with their long beaks and the tips of their tongues to lap up the nectar within the tubes. In doing so, pollen attaches to their feathery breasts, which they then carry off to pollinate other gilias.

You'll also find the shrubby looking, 1–3′ tall plants of Tahoe Lupine (*Lupinus argenteus* var. *meionanthus*). It has white, silvery haired leaves and blue, ⅜″ wide flowers. The upper banner petal is spotted with either white or yellow, and its sepals are shaggy haired, like a shaggy little beard that grows out of its "chin." Two wing petals hide a tiny keel that houses its reproductive parts. See p. 11.

Those hiking in May or early June, soon after the snow melts, will find the small, pink, ground-carpeting flowers of Steer's Head, which resemble cow skulls on a desert floor. The cushion plants of Butterballs with red to white flowers and tiny leaves are also early bloomers at high elevations. Cushion plants grow low to the ground for protection from fierce winds at high elevations. Early-season hikers will also find the similar looking Globe Gilia with white flowers and tiny, fan-shaped leaves. But the cutest of all will be Pursh's Woolly Pod (*Astragalus purshii*) with small, rosy purple pea flowers that grow just above woolly, white leaves. It is also an early bloomer

Pursh's Woolly Pod

with a long blooming period. While it is in flower, it will also be setting fruit from the flowers that have already bloomed. The fruits are charming, woolly seedpods, which sometimes resemble little tails of Cottontail Rabbits.

Beyond the Sentinels in an Alpine Habitat

After leaving the open slopes, you'll arrive at more saddles with similar views down to the Kirkwood Ski Resort. The purple, 4-petaled flowers of **Dagger Pod** grow about 2–8″ tall with downy soft leaves. It's named for its 2½″ long, flattened, dagger-shaped fruit. It's a common plant at Tahoe's high elevations that migrated up the eastern slope of the Sierra Nevada from the Great Basin.

Dagger Pod

In open, grassy meadows or by forest openings, look for the ground hugging Meadow or Dinnerplate Thistle (*Cirsium scariosum* var. *americanum*). Each plant has one or more clusters of white disk flowers that sit in the center of a basal rosette of leaves, which are lobed and spine tipped. They are hairy or glabrous on the surface and densely matted with gray hairs on the underside. Native Americans consumed the buds of these thistles, just as we do with artichoke thistles.

Dagger Pod fruit

Meadow Thistle

Blue Flax

Blue Flax is a striking plant that grows 2′ tall, with 1–1½″ wide, blue flowers. Each flower blooms for less than a day and in late afternoon, its petals fall off and flutter to the ground like small, blue butterflies. Each day new flowers appear. When you find several of these plants growing together, stop for a moment and look closely at the flowers to see if you notice a difference between them. Though the flowers appear the same in most respects, you'll discover that in some the style is very long, while in other flowers the style is short. This condition is called "heterostyly," which means "different styles."

On other hikes, I've discussed some of the structural mechanisms that have evolved in flowers to help reduce self-pollination; the heterostyly of the Blue Flax is another such mechanism. It works this way: the short-styled flowers produce large pollen grains, which are incompatible with the stigma of their own short-styled flowers. Therefore, pollen inadvertently brushed onto its own stigma will not cause self-pollination. Long-styled flowers, which produce small pollen grains, can only fertilize the short-styled flowers.

Prickly Phlox

After fertilization occurs, shiny brown seeds are produced that are rich in oil. It is from a related species of flax that we extract linseed oil. Flax has long been important for its fiber, as well as for its seeds, and has been in cultivation since ancient times. "Linum" is derived from the Greek "linon" for thread. Native Americans roasted and consumed the seeds and made an eye medicine from the soaked roots.

Prickly Phlox (*Linanthus pungens*) lives among the rocks. It has a pungent fragrance and grows from

4–12″ tall with palmate leaves that are spine-tipped. If you place your open palm down on top of the leaves, you'll know how it got its name. If you confuse this plant with the non-prickly Spreading Phlox, just do the palm test, and you'll be able to tell the difference. The flowers of Prickly Phlox are white to a light pink on the surface of its flaring petals. The flower petals fuse to form a long tube, and the underside of the petals is white, lavender or pinkish. Its anthers are very tiny and golden and hide down in the flowers.

Mount Rose Wild Buckwheat

After Passing Martin Point

The trail continues through a forest on several switchbacks and along the east side of 9,260′ Martin Point, until it reaches an open ridgeline with the small plant, **Mount Rose Wild Buckwheat**, which was "first" discovered at Tahoe on Mount Rose. It's only 1–6″ tall with red buds that open to form yellow flowers. Its leaves are very fuzzy and rise vertically. Another hairy-leaved plant with yellow flowers is the **Woolly Groundsel**, which generally lives at elevations above 8,500′ in dry, rocky habitats. Its few ray flowers (petals) surround golden disk flowers that seem to be "exuberantly" preparing to bloom while some disk flowers in the center may still be tightly in bud. See pp. 112–113. You'll also find the 6–8″ tall Shining Fleabane (*Erigeron barbellulatus*) that blooms nearby in groups with lavender or white daisies. Its cheery flowers greet hikers who stop to say hello as they leave the ridgeline to start up the trail to the mountaintop.

Woolly Groundsel

The final ridgeline that is reached, before you head up to the gap in Thunder Mountain's pinnacles, is so wide open that heavy winds usually blow hard across the flower slopes. Off in the distance, you'll see the majestic, jagged pinnacles on the volcanic ridgeline that hides Thunder Mountain. On the left is a prominent, dark spire with a

Shining Fleabane

gap in the pinnacles, which is where the trail passes through to head down and around the south side and west to reach the path up to Thunder Mountain's summit.

Dwarf Monkeyflower

Before continuing up the trail, while you are still on the level part, zip up your jacket and wander down the grassy slope below to get out of the wind and look for the 1–6″ tall **Dwarf Monkeyflower**. It blooms with pink or yellow flowers in damp rocky areas or among the grasses. Each little blossom gazes upward innocently with a cute little expression. After admiring it, see if you can find its tiny stigma that opens and closes when touched with pollen, as discussed on the Castle Valley hike. See p. 96.

Alpine Cryptantha

Back on the trail, you'll find Alpine Cryptantha (*Cryptantha humilis*), which is another plant that prefers exposed ridgelines and elevations above 8,000′. Its flowers are white with a golden, raised ring in the center, and the leaves are very hairy, like a warm sweater. The dense hairs slow down the movement of air across the leaf surface, which reduces evaporation of water from the leaves. The dense hairs also reflect intense sunlight to protect delicate plant tissue from being damaged by the sun.

In dry, rocky habitats you'll find the 6–18″ tall Hot-rock Penstemon (*Penstemon deustus*), which is Tahoe's only white to creamy colored Penstemon, making it easy to identify. Brown nectar lines mark the lower petals, and its small, tubular flowers grow in whorls along the upper stem. Its staminode (stamen without an anther) is glabrous at the tip. See p. 125. The tough coating on its leathery leaves helps to conserve moisture in its dry

Hot-rock Penstemon

habitat. Indians dried the roots and ground them into a powder, which they applied to their gums to relieve toothaches. They also used the leaves in a soothing eyewash solution.

Look also for the Cut-leaf Fleabane (*Erigeron compositus*), a low growing plant up to 6″ tall, with densely packed, hairy leaves. Its white ray flowers surround yellow disk flowers in the center. Fleabane's flowers nod in bud and appear pink initially, but as the flowers open, the ray flowers elongate and become white. Their stems also straighten to show off the beauty of their flowers and to announce their availability to pollinators.

Cut-leaf Fleabane

In open, moist, coniferous forests, the California Valerian (*Valeriana californica*) grows from 8–20″ tall with flowers that are pinkish in bud and white in flower. If the flowers have gone to seed, be sure to use your hand lens to view their feathery styles that are delicate, spreading, and on top of the seeds. The styles help distribute the tender seeds in the wind. The strong smelling roots of the Valerian were dried and made into a tea by Native Americans to be taken as a sedative. Valerian capsules made from the roots are available for this use in natural food stores.

California Valerian

Valerian's seeds with feathery styles

Nearby look for the white, daisy-like flowers of Yarrow (*Achillea millefolium*). "Millefolium" or a "thousand leaves," refers to its numerous, pinnate leaves and finely dissected leaflets. It grows about 6–18″ tall with flowers that appear to be Umbels, but if you look closely, you'll see that their stems grow along the upper stem, instead of radiating outward from *one* central point,

Yarrow

Nancy Gilbert

Variable Checkerspot on Yarrow

Sierra Primrose

Timberline Phacelia

like the members of the Umbel Family. Native Americans and other herbalists have also used Yarrow for generations to stop external bleeding from wounds. It is an astringent, which causes blood to clot by constricting the blood vessels when its freshly crushed leaves are applied to open wounds.

Climbing up to the Backside for the Summit

After leaving ridgeline gardens, you'll head up to the gap on switchbacks that pass gorgeous, pink Sierra Primroses (*Primula suffretescens*) along the rocky trail. Their bright yellow centers make the flowers glow even brighter. Their evergreen leaves are covered with snow all winter, but as it melts, they have a head start on photosynthesizing. When the trail levels out by the gap, you'll be rewarded for your climb in June with groups of the low-growing plants and beautiful, blue flowers of the Showy Polemonium. After passing through the gap, the trail heads past slopes of Sulphur Flowers, Stickseeds, Wavey-leaved Paintbrushes, and the Timberline Phacelia (*Phacelia hastata* ssp. *compacta*). Its flowers are either lavender or white and are coiled like fuzzy caterpillars that snuggle in their densely hairy leaves.

The trail then arrives at a junction with the Horse Canyon Trail. Continue along the main trail as it follows the contours of the mountain for about 0.25 mile to an unsigned junction. Leave the trail there and turn right onto the path that heads up a 0.6-mile climb through scattered trees to the rocky summit of Thunder Mountain. The summit is thrilling with brisk, clean air and far-ranging mountain vistas. You'll see the distant peaks of Yosemite to the south, Desolation Wilderness to the north, and local views of Round Top Mountain, Carson Pass, and the Caples and Silver Lakes below. You will want to linger here awhile to enjoy your accomplishment and to bathe in the pure sunlight and pure air.

A blissful Marmot basks in late afternoon light   *A peaceful Marmot overlooks a meadow*

Heading Back Down

When you are ready to head back, you'll have the pleasure of knowing that the trail is generally downhill, as you again pass through beautiful flower gardens that may now be glowing in the low-angled, late afternoon light. While you are heading out, keep your eyes open for the Marmots that live here. One afternoon, as I was walking down the trail, I was surprised to see a Marmot standing upright with its little arms stretched forward, basking in the warmth and glow of the late afternoon light. It was spellbound, as it raised its chin upward to catch a bit more light. I quickly snapped a picture, before it saw me and headed off into the rocks. It's always a pleasure to find a Marmot peacefully resting on a rock looking out over the flowers and to the mountains beyond, but I never had the pleasure of experiencing one standing up in a state of bliss. We never know what we're going to find at the next bend in the trail!

Mountain Pride decorates rock-strewn slopes

Saying Good-bye

As our journey together comes to an end, I want to thank you for sharing it with me. After spending this time in Tahoe's wild gardens, I hope that you've enjoyed the richness of yourself as well as the beauty of Tahoe's wildflowers.

When our hearts are open, the study of wildflowers is not "just botany," and hiking is not "just exercise" but rather a path for self-discovery —a means to explore our inner selves to find wholeness. For as John Muir once said, "I only went out for a walk and finally concluded to stay out till sundown, for going out, I found, was really going in."

I too plan to stay out till sundown, so if you are out hiking one day and come upon a woman with a blue hat, kneeling down happily examining a new flower, I hope you'll come on over and say hello!

Glossary

anther: pollen producing part of male stamen

appressed: lying flat against a surface

axil: point in upper angle of leaf stem off a main stem

banner petal: the upright petal on a pea flower

basal leaves: located at or near a stem's base

belly plant: term for small plants best viewed on one's belly

binary key: a system using two options in a flower key

bisexual flower: with both male and female reproductive parts

bracts: small leaf-like structures below a flower or along a stem

buzz-pollinated: occurs when a bee vibrates its wings to release pollen

calyx: collective term for sepals

catkin: a spike of either female or male flowers, often without petals

chaparral: dense thickets of drought-tolerant, fire-adapted shrubs

chloroplast: plant cells of chlorophyll where photosynthesis occurs

cleistogamous: self-fertilization in plants with permanently closed flowers

compound leaf: leaf divided into separate, smaller parts called leaflets

conifer: evergreen trees with either needle-shaped or scale-like leaves and cones with naked seeds

cushion plant: plant that grows compactly and low to the ground

deciduous: on trees, leaves that fall off seasonally, usually in winter, and can refer to flower parts also

dioecious: plant that produces male and female flowers on separate plants

disk flower: tubular, 5-petaled flower in the Sunflower Family

fascicle: a tiny, brown, papery sheath that encloses a bundle of pine needles

filament: the often thread-like part of a stamen that holds the anther

fruit: an ovary that swells with seeds as it matures after fertilization

gall: structure formed on plant parts to house insect eggs and larvae

glabrous: without hairs

glands: tiny round, secreting cells on surface of leaves, stems, flowers

glandular hair: small round tip of hair that exudes a sticky substance

glaucous: waxy film on plant stems or parts, which can be rubbed off

haustoria: specialized parasitic roots that penetrate neighboring plants

hemi-parasite: a plant that photosynthesizes and is also a parasite

inflorescence: cluster of flowers

leaflet: separate smaller leaves that make up a compound leaf

monoecious: separate male and female flowers on same plant

moraine: accumulation of rocks and soil, deposited by glaciers

myco-heterotroph: plants parasitic or dependent on soil fungi to live

mycorrhizae: a symbiotic union between plants and the soil fungi that coat or penetrate the plants' roots. Plants exude carbohydrates and other nutrients from their root tips in exchange for water and nutrients from the soil fungi. At least 90% of all plants live by this relationship.

Nature: the vast, mysterious, life force

nature: the forms by which Nature expresses herself

nectar gland: plant organ that creates sweet nectar

node: swelling on stem where sub-stems, leaves, flowers originate

ovary: base of pistil that houses ovules and maturing seeds

ovule: an egg before it becomes a seed after fertilization

palmate leaf: three or more leaflets that radiate from a central point

pappus: hairy-like bristles attached to seeds in Sunflower Family

phyllaries: leafy bracts that encircle flowers of Sunflower Family

pinnate leaf: leaf with leaflets arranged in two flat rows along mid-vein

pistil: female reproductive part made up of ovary, style, and stigma

plant embryo: a young developing plant inside a seed

pollinia: a mass of pollen grains on an anther, transported by pollinators

proboscis: tube-like, flexible mouthpart to suck nectar

ray flower: single, petal flower in the Sunflower Family

rhizoid: root hair

rhizome: underground horizontal stem

sepals: a leafy structure that surrounds a flower in bud

stamen: flower's male reproductive part made up of a filament and an anther

staminate flower: with male reproductive parts only

staminode: a filament without an anther

stigma: tip of pistil that receives pollen

style: stalk that connects ovary and stigma

tubular flower: a flower with petals fused below, forming a tube

umbel-shaped flower: flower stems that radiate from central point on a main stem

whorl: three of more leaves or flowers surrounding a node or stem

Acknowledgments

I'm grateful to Rondal Snodgrass for his helpful editorial input. He also hiked the trails with me, carried the heavy pack, and made it even more fun to be among the wildflowers. I'm grateful for my children, Jennifer Rosser and Michael Carville, for their enduring love and support and for my grandchildren, Cooper and Aurora, who love wildflowers, bugs, and being in the wild.

Joan Keyes and Jonathan Peck of Dovetail Publishing Services are a delight. Their professionalism and Joan's fabulous design and typographic abilities brought the book to life. Carole Quandt and Ken Hassman contributed their expertise, and Jeff Major and Dome Printing did a great job. Alicia Funk helped in the early stage.

Roger Rosenberger, Lisa Berry, Steve Ashcraft, and Geoff Griffin contributed their beautiful photos, and showed me new wildflower trails. Tanja Aminoff, Hilary and Garth D'Attilo, Janelle Bloomdale, Jim Fowler, Ames and Nancy Gilbert, Roger McGehee, and Rondal Snodgrass also contributed photos to enrich the book. Charly Price created the fine maps.

I also appreciate the enthusiastic support of Julie Becker, Mary Jane Di Piero, Kathleen Fenton, Mano, Carolyn Singer, Christina Slowick, Wendy Thompson, Melony Vance, Karen Wiese, Carl Wishner, and Carla Woodside. Laird Blackwell was there in the beginning sharing a love for the wildflowers.

I'm grateful for the pollinators who sustain life on this planet. I honor the trees who appeared on earth long before we did; without them, we wouldn't be here or be sheltered by their beauty.

And, finally, I want to give my special thanks to all the wildflowers, for they were the ones who showed me the way back to myself and made the process so much fun!

264

About the Author

Julie Carville is a botanist, naturalist, and photographer. She is the author of *Lingering in Tahoe's Wild Gardens*, 1989, and its later edition, *Hiking Tahoe's Wildflower Trails*, 1997. She is a co-author of *Wildflowers of Nevada & Placer Counties, California*, 2008; *Trees and Shrubs of Nevada & Placer Counties, California*, 2014; and a contributing author of *California's Wild Gardens*, 1997.

Roger McGehee

She has written and photographed for numerous publications, including the *Sacramento Bee*, *Sierra Heritage* magazine, and the *San Francisco Chronicle*. For many years, she authored a weekly wildflower column for the *Tahoe World* and *Sierra Sun* newspapers, writing about the beauty of Tahoe's wildflowers, its trails, and Native American plant knowledge. She is a co-founder and past president of the Tahoe Chapter of the California Native Plant Society (CNPS) and a co-founder of the Nevada County Redbud Chapter.

Her love of Nature began as a child and was deepened by years of backpacking, skiing, and a move to Tahoe. She created Mountain Gypsy Wildflower Seminars, and for 40 years has led wildflower field classes for private groups, environmental organizations, and colleges. Through this, she has experienced the profound effect that experiences in Nature have on both children and adults.

She helped develop and lead classes for the California State Parks *Women in the Outdoors* program, which encouraged women to hike, camp, and enjoy the outdoors with confidence. As an instructor for the California State Parks Whitewater Recreation Office, she taught wildflower and interpretive training classes for educators and river guides.

Julie has also traveled throughout Northern California presenting programs on California's native plants for public institutions and private groups. In 2014, the Bear Yuba Land Trust recognized her work with the John Skinner Outdoors Recreation Award.

Bibliography

Abram, David. 2011. *Becoming Animal: An Earthly Cosmology*. New York, NY: Vintage Books, Random House, Inc.

Anderson, M. Kat. 2006. *Tending the Wild: Native American Knowledge and Management of California's Natural Resources*. Berkeley, Los Angeles & London: University of California Press.

Baldwin, Bruce G., Douglas H. Goldman, David J. Keil, Robert Patterson, Thomas J. Rosatti, & Dieter H. Wilken [Eds]. 2012. *The Jepson Manual: Vascular Plants of California*. 2nd edition. Berkeley & Los Angeles, CA: University of California Press.

Beedy, Edward C. & Pandolfino, Edward R. *Birds of the Sierra Nevada: Their Natural History, Status, and Distribution*. Berkeley & Los Angeles, CA: University of California Press.

Blackwell, Laird R. 1999. *Wildflowers of the Sierra Nevada and the Central Valley*. Vancouver, BC, Canada: Lone Pine Publishing.

Buffagni, Silvia. 2014. *The Music of the Plants*. Italy: Devodama.

Buhner, Stephen Harrod. 2014. *Plant Intelligence and the Imaginal Realm*. Rochester, Vermont: Bear & Company.

Carson, Rachel. 1956. *The Sense of Wonder*. New York, NY: Harper & Row.

Eiseley, Loren. 1957. *The Immense Journey*. 6th edition. New York NY: Vintage Books, Random House.

Eiseley, Loren. 1996. *How Flowers Changed the World*. San Francisco, CA: Sierra Club Books.

Graf, Michael. 1999. *Plants of the Tahoe Basin: Flowering Plants, Trees, and Ferns*. Sacramento, CA: California Native Plant Society Press, & Berkeley & Los Angeles, CA: University of California Press.

Lanner, Ronald M. 1999. *Conifers of California*. Los Olivos, CA: Cachuma Press.

Laws, John Muir. 2007. *The Laws Field Guide to the Sierra Nevada*. Berkeley, CA: Heyday Books.

Leopold, Aldo. 1970. *A Sand County Almanac: With Essays on Conservation from Round River*. New York: Ballantine Books.

Redbud Chapter. 2007. *Wildflowers of Nevada and Placer Counties, California.* Sacramento, CA: California Native Plant Society, Sacramento, CA.

Redbud Chapter. 2014. *Trees and Shrubs of Nevada and Placer Counties, California,* Nevada City, CA: Redbud Chapter, in association with the California Native Plant Society, Sacramento, CA.

Russo, Ron. 2006. *A Field Guide to Plant Galls of California and Other Western States.* Berkeley & Los Angeles, CA: University of California Press.

Schaffer, Jeffrey P. 1998. *The Tahoe Sierra: A Natural History Guide to 112 Hikes in the Northern Sierra.* 4th edition. Berkeley, CA: Wilderness Press.

Storer, Tracy I., Robert L. Usinger, & David Lukas. 2004. *Sierra Nevada Natural History.* Revised edition. Berkeley & Los Angeles, CA & London: University of California Press.

Wiese, Karen. *Sierra Nevada Wildflowers: Including Yosemite, Sequoia, and Kings Canyon National Parks.* 2013. Guilford, CT: Globe Pequot Press.

Websites

The **California Native Plant Society** (CNPS) is a statewide, non-profit organization of amateurs and professionals with a common interest in California's native plants. It seeks to increase understanding of California's native flora and to preserve this rich resource for future generations. Membership is open to all (www.cnps.org).

Local Chapters:
Tahoe Chapter (www.tahoecnps.org)
Redbud Chapter (www.redbud-cnps.org)

The **Consortium of California Herbaria** serves as a gateway to information from California vascular plant specimens that are housed in participant herbaria. Their database includes over 2 million specimen records from 35 institutions (ucjeps.berkeley.edu/consortium).

Plant Name Updates: www.ucjeps.berkeley.edu/interchange

Photos of California Plants:
www.calphotos.berkeley.edu/flora
www.calflora.org

Cushion plants on Castle Peak's flanks

Index

NOTE: **Bolded** page numbers indicate featured flowers. *Italicized* page numbers indicate a photo or hike map.

Ooops, below are some corrections

Copyright page iv: The cover photo caption should read "Trail up Basin Peak."

p. 14: Title should read "Are Plants Intelligent?"

p. 27, add: "In the 'Flowers by Color' section, use the flower's common name to search the Index for its Latin or botanical name."

p. 33: The photo in the bottom row labeled "Rocky Mountain Butterweed" is actually "Rabbitbrush." See p. 115 for the Rocky Mountain Butterweed photo and description.

p. 36: Pussypaws flowers also bloom white.

p. 50, end of first paragraph: Change "See p. 99" to "See top of p. 79."

p. 222, second paragraph, please note: Bumblebees buzz-pollinate the elephant's head flowers. They do so by disengaging their flight muscles from their wings, so they won't take flight. They then very rapidly vibrate the muscles, as they grab the flower, which causes their bodies to shake so violently that the enclosed pollen, which is hidden inside the anther, floats out from the anther's tiny holes to dust the bees body. Potatoes, blueberries, pumpkins, zucchinis, and wildflowers of manzanitas, shooting stars, and mountain bluebells are among the flowers that are buzz-pollinated. Only a small number of flower species are pollinated by the insects who know how to use this amazing technique. Honeybees lack this skill.

p. 255, second paragraph: Change "See pp. 112–113" to "See pp. 154–155."

p. 262, change Glossary definition: buzz-pollinated: A pollination technique used by bumblebees, and some other insects, to release pollen that is hidden and enclosed in the anthers of some flower species. See p. 222.